# Ireland

## Land of Opportunity for Investment, Business, Residence, and Retirement

by

Adam Starchild

**Fredonia Books**
**Amsterdam, The Netherlands**

Ireland:
Land of Opportunity for Investment, Business,
Residence, and Retirement

by
Adam Starchild

ISBN: 1-4101-0886-4

Fredonia Books
Amsterdam, The Netherlands
http://www.fredoniabooks.com

# Contents

i

# Introduction

# The Republic of Ireland — New Land of Opportunity

When people think of Ireland, few think of the country as a place to start a business, make investments, emigrate to in search of a better life, or retire to in hopes of spending golden years in delightful activities and pursuits. These people don't realize that Ireland possesses an exceptionally high quality of life, low living costs, low crime, and low stress. Without question, Ireland is becoming a most attractive island on which to live.

The Republic of Ireland, which includes by far the greatest part of the island of Ireland, boasts a scenic, unspoiled environment that is steeped in lore and history. Called *Eire* in Gaelic, the country's traditional language, Ireland has been invaded several times during the last 2,000 years, resulting in a modern Irish culture that is a fascinating blend of the legacies of Celts, English, Vikings, and Normans.

There is far more to Ireland, however, than just culture. Ireland has evolved into Europe's most important offshore financial center, leading to a host of significant advantages to investors. Through the establishment of a non-resident company in Ireland, investors are able to realize an excellent return on their investment, reduce their taxes, and secure their privacy. Individuals can receive tax benefits even if they live in Ireland only a few months out of each year, and business conducted offshore is not subject to tax, provided there is no income arising from operations within Ireland.

People seeking a superior land for retirement often find Ireland an excellent choice. Along with Ireland's fine investment climate, retirees enjoy free hospitalization, free transportation on buses and trains, and, in some cases, even free fuel and energy. Retirees also find the price of land and housing in Ireland to be most reasonable, and they genuinely appreciate Ireland's low rate of crime. Many people moving to Ireland feel safer in their new homes than just about anywhere else they lived.

For those wishing to stay in Ireland at least part of the year, or who would like to obtain residency, Ireland is relatively easy to enter. This is particularly true if you have an Irish ancestor, and in many cases you need not have descended from this individual in a direct line.

Ireland has changed remarkably in the last several years, achieving a style of living that is both comfortable and rewarding, but it is likely that the nation's future will be even brighter. During the last two decades the Irish government has invested in infrastructure and telecommunications in an effort to position the country to take part in the grand global economy. The success of this policy is obvious in Ireland's steady economic gains. Furthermore, Ireland is poised to benefit from the investment of overseas companies even as its own economy continues to expand. Strong, consistent growth is expected well into the future.

All this makes Ireland an extremely attractive place for relocation, retirement, and investment. Ireland, clearly, has much to offer just about everyone.

# The Land Called Ireland

The Republic of Ireland, which occupies five-sixths of the island of Ireland, is the second largest island in the British Isles. The remaining one-sixth of the island is occupied by Northern Ireland, which is a part of the United Kingdom. If measured from north to south, the entire island is about 300 miles (485 kilometers). From west to east it is about 174 miles (280 kilometers). The Republic of Ireland should not be confused with Northern Ireland, which has been plagued by violence between Protestants and Catholics for generations. Compared to Northern Ireland, the Republic of Ireland is a tranquil and secure country.

The Republic of Ireland, hereafter referred to as simply Ireland, covers about 27,136 square miles (about 70,280 kilometers). The westernmost of the British Isles, Ireland is separated from the rest of Great Britain by the Irish Sea. While the Atlantic Ocean surrounds Ireland on the north, west, and south, Wales, Scotland, and England lie about 50 miles (about 80 kilometers) to the east.

# Topography

Most of Ireland is a low-lying island with small mountain ranges that tend to roll, rather than thrust upward. Much of the land is covered with lush vegetation. This is particularly true of the island's coasts and valleys. Low mountain ranges and a fertile central plain are the island's dominant features. Some of the country's best farmland is found on the central plain, especially around the Shannon River, which winds through the fruitful interior, providing water for some of the nation's finest farms.

Ireland has many low mountain ranges. The most rugged are the Wicklow Mountains located south of Dublin, and the mountains of County Kerry on the southwest coast. Carrantuohill, the island's highest peak at 3,414 feet (1,041 meters), is found here. Most of the mountains that surround the central plain are devoid of much vegetation, while the mountains along Ireland's western coast are windswept and rocky. Steep cliffs rise up from the shoreline and above the small islands that mark this region. Ireland's eastern coast is also highlighted by mountains, though none of the peaks rival Carrantuohill.

Ireland contains many rivers. The Shannon River, its source in the northwestern part of the island, flows through mountains and plains for over 230 miles, eventually emptying into the Atlantic on Ireland's western coast. The Shannon's mouth opens into the bay on which the port of Limerick is located. Another major river is the Liffey, which begins in the Wicklow Mountains and flows to the northeast through Dublin and into the Irish Sea. Other important rivers include the Nore, Suir, and Lee which flow through southeastern Ireland and the Moy that flows in the northwest. Numerous smaller rivers and rivulets mark the countryside. Ireland also possesses several lakes. Much of the land remains clean and unpolluted, and many environmentalists believe Ireland to be the most pollution-free country in all of Europe.

# Climate

Because Ireland lies in the path of the Gulf Stream, a warm ocean current that begins in the Western Hemisphere's equatorial regions, the island's climate is more moderate than other places at similar latitudes. The climate also is marked by less variation than one would expect it to have.

Overall, Ireland's climate is wet and mild. Because the island is small, all parts of it are affected by the sea. As a result, Ireland's summers tend to be cool and its winters mild. Average summer temperatures range between 57 and 68 degrees F (about 14 to 20 degrees C), and average winter temperatures hover between 40 and 45 degrees F (about 4 to 7 degrees C). Ireland receives about 40 inches (100 centimeters) of rainfall each year with all seasons receiving an ample amount of precipitation. The regular rainfall results in Ireland's fertile soils being quite productive, particularly in river valleys.

## Vegetation

As recent as 5,000 B.C., a land bridge connected Ireland to mainland Europe. Once this land bridge disappeared, animals could no longer migrate to Ireland from Europe, limiting the variety of animal life found on the island. The variety of plant life was similarly affected. Although the types of plants may have been reduced, the lushness of Ireland was not affected by the loss of the land bridge. Because of Ireland's plentiful rainfall, the island's natural vegetation is thick and lush, giving rise to the nickname of the Emerald Isle.

Once, before the arrival of great numbers of people, Ireland was covered almost entirely with thick forests. Indeed, in some parts of the island, forests of birch, ash, hazel, oak, alder, and willow trees predominate the local environment. Killarney Valley, which is the site of one of the island's long-standing forests, is noted for its mosses and ferns. Today, forests account for just under 4% of the island's land area.

Marshes are found throughout the island, and within them a variety of ferns and bushes abound. Rhododendrons and fuchsia grow wild over many bogs, painting the land with vivid colors hard to match. When its plants are abloom, Ireland is truly an island of enchantment.

## Ireland's People

About 3.5 million people live in the Republic of Ireland. Close to 95% of the nation's population are Roman Catholics with much of the remainder belonging to Protestant churches. This is in contrast to Northern Ireland (which is a part of the United Kingdom) where the population is predominately Protestant.

The great majority of Ireland's population has descended from the Celts, thought by some historians to be among the island's earliest inhabitants. Some of the country's people have descended from the English, but these are a small percentage. Many Irish people have at least some Scandinavian and Norman blood, a result of invasions that occurred several hundred years ago. No significant minorities live in Ireland.

About 50% of Ireland's people are younger than 28, making the country's population one of the youngest and fastest growing among the countries of Europe. This segment of the population, which is highly educated, ensures an efficient workforce for the future which will be the foundation of the nation's economy.

Although Gaelic is Ireland's traditional language, almost all the Irish people speak English, which is by far the most common language spoken in the country. English is the language of commerce, business, and tourism. Virtually all of Ireland's workforce speaks English, which, along with Irish, is an official language of the country.

# Ireland's Cities

More than 50% of Ireland's people reside in cities and large towns. Over 470,00 people live in Dublin, the capital city, about 125,000 live in Cork, and about 80,000 live in Limerick. Other cities, which in fact are more like large towns, include Waterford, Killarney, Galway, and Kilkenny.

Dublin is Ireland's most prestigious city. It is a business, manufacturing, and cultural center. The city's streets are wide and clean, dotted with public squares and delightful parks. Divided by the Liffey River and connected to the Shannon River by the Grand and Royal canals, which in the past served as prime routes for commerce, Dublin is a picturesque city that in many ways is the center of life in Ireland.

Along with its importance as a site for commerce and culture, Dublin is home to the Trinity College, also known as the University of Dublin. Founded in 1592, the university is testament to a long history of support for education and contains one of the largest libraries in the world. A major goal of the public education system is to prepare Irish students for higher education in one of the nation's seven universities, nine regional colleges, and eleven colleges specializing in technology. The colleges that hold technology at the heart of their curriculums indicate the future-looking perspective of the educational establishment. It is clear that an understanding and mastery of technology are keys to economic development in the global economy and emphasis is placed upon these areas.

After Dublin, Cork is the second most populous city in Ireland with more than 150,000 residents. Situated on Ireland's southern coast, Cork's harbor is a commercial hub, handling great numbers of ships. The city is also a center for shipbuilding. Rail lines transport imported products, particularly grains, to the island's interior, and carry cattle, dairy products, bacon, and eggs for export. Other industries in and around Cork include iron foundries, textile mills, breweries, and factories for the production of chemical manures, gloves, and leather goods.

Limerick, with a population of about 80,000, is located on Ireland's western coast and serves as an industrial and agricultural center for its region. It is also an important port. Major industries include textile and flower mills and factories that produce foodstuffs.

Many other small cities and towns — Galway, Waterford, Kilkenny and Tipperary are some — have their own delights and enchantments and usually derive their economic activity from regional industries including small-scale manufacturing, brewing ale and beer, and dairy products.

# History

Ireland's history begins more than 5000 years ago. Since those times, the island has been invaded by Celts, Scandinavians (Vikings), Normans, and English. All of these groups have left a mark on Irish culture, which is unique and distinct to the island.

The first people living in Ireland were a Mesolithic race of hunters and gatherers. Little is known about them. Legends tell of several independent groups, including Nemedians, Fomorians, and Firbolgs. Old stories tell how these tribes fought among themselves and also against tribes of Scots, thought to have been called Milesians.

By about 3000 B.C. these original inhabitants of the island were overcome by Neolithic invaders from Europe. Much of what researchers know about these people comes from their burial sites. They placed items such as weapons, jewelry, pottery, and bone implements inside their tombs, which often were little more than earthen mounds located on hilltops. These artifacts are similar to the kinds found throughout Great Britain and Europe, indicating that these early Irish were members of a larger group. At first they appeared to be primarily hunters and gatherers, however, they gradually learned to farm, and by 2000 B.C. cultivation was rather widespread. Metal artifacts dating from this time have also been found, evidence that the early Irish became good metalworkers. Similar artifacts from the same general period are found throughout Europe, providing a strong argument that the Irish maintained trading ties with other people.

The early Irish were largely left alone until Celtic tribes began expanding throughout Europe. Coming from northeastern Europe around 350 B.C., the Celts, a rugged, warlike people, moved through France and Spain, eventually crossing what was to become the English Channel and overrunning the land that would one day be called England. It wasn't long afterward that tribes of Celts that called themselves Gaels reached Ireland, in time taking control of the island and spreading their language, customs, and culture. They called their new land Eire. History hasn't conclusively revealed what happened to the earlier inhabitants of Ireland, though most researchers assume that they were either killed or absorbed by the Celts.

Unlike many conquerors throughout history who seize lands as a unified force, it is likely that the Celts' conquest was slow and piecemeal. Indeed, the Celts seemed not to have one all-powerful ruler, but instead had many leaders, each controlling his own kingdom. This kingdom was called a *tuatha*, and consisted of people who shared a common ancestor. The greatest amount of power in a tuatha was wielded by the nobility or upper class, which chose a chief. In addition to the upper class, tuathas contained priests, called Druids, and commoners. Most Celtic tribes valued their independence and the individual tribes remained in a near constant state of warfare against their neighbors.

By some accounts, it took the tribes hundreds of years to finally divide Ireland into five major kingdoms: Munster, Connaught, Meath, Leinster, and Ulster. It wasn't until about 380 A.D. that a single ruler was able to unite most of Ireland. Niall of the Nine Hostages, who got his name by taking hostages from the tuatha he gained control of, ruled Ireland for about 25 years.

While the Celtic tribes fought each other in Ireland, Christianity was spreading through much of western Europe.

In 432, with the arrival of St. Patrick, Christianity reached Ireland. Patrick assumed the mission of founding numerous churches in Ireland and bringing the faith to many of the Celts. Monasteries sprang up throughout Ireland, many of them establishing schools that began turning out monks and missionaries. By the sixth century Irish monasteries had developed into centers of learning that taught both academic subjects as well as religion, and Irish missionaries were journeying to England and Europe. Irish monks created many works of art and much literature, one of the most famous manuscripts being the *Book of Kells*, which is a copy of the Christian Gospels.

Around the beginning of the ninth century, Vikings — raiders from Scandinavia — began plundering towns along the Irish coast. Adventuresome, fearless, and barbaric, the Vikings were lured by Ireland's wealth, and they soon began sailing up Ireland's rivers into the island's interior where they wrecked havoc on towns and monasteries. Eventually some of Vikings settled in Ireland and founded some of Ireland's most noted cities, including Dublin, Cork, and Limerick.

Near the middle part of the ninth century, Irish chiefs managed to unite against the Viking raiders, but it was not until 1014 that the Irish, under their king Brian Boru, were able to defeat the Vikings at the Battle of Clontarf.

Unfortunately, Boru was killed in the battle and the Irish chiefs quickly began feuding among themselves once more.

Although many Vikings, especially those given to warfare, were forced from Ireland, many others who had settled remained and were eventually absorbed into Ireland's predominately Celtic population. Despite being absorbed, the Vikings had a lasting effect on Ireland. Because of their affinity for the sea, many Viking groups established coastal communities, which were naturally interested in trade with overseas lands. Their vision helped to build and maintain early trade.

For a time, until the early 1100s, the Irish enjoyed relative peace, fighting only against each other. As the twelfth century approached, however, a new threat came to the island. The Normans, who had conquered England in 1066, now moved on Ireland.

Originally from Normandy in France, the Normans of the early twelfth century were probably Europe's most effective fighting force. Disciplined, well-trained, and accustomed to fighting as units, the Normans brought with them advanced weapons, including iron swords, powerful crossbows, and strong war horses. They also arrived with the highest confidence. The disunited and quarreling Irish armies were little match for them.

By 1250 the Normans controlled much of Ireland and had introduced feudalism, an economic system in which the king owned all the land, parcels of which he in turn would grant to nobles who pledged to him their loyalty and service. The nobles would then grant portions of their land to underlings who either worked the land themselves or granted portions of their holdings to others to farm. This system introduced a rather rigid social system, control over which was exercised by the nobility which itself was dependent upon the king for its power and holdings. The Normans also established their legal system throughout Ireland, modeled on the system which they had established in England.

Irish chiefs periodically rose up and tried to regain their power, but they had little success. This changed, however, when Norman nobles who had lived in Ireland for generations began to side with the Irish against English kings who they felt were insensitive to their needs. The English kings tried to limit the power of the Irish by passing laws — one, for example, forbade the Irish to buy weapons — but the Irish and Irish-Normans continued to seek greater freedom from England. By the early 1400s, the area of Ireland that England controlled, called the Pale, was limited to the eastern part of the island centered around Dublin.

The struggle of the Irish against the English crown continued through the next several centuries. Despite Irish protests and occasional rebellions, Britain stubbornly held on. In time, some of the Irish became members of the Church of England, often pitting them against their Catholic Irish neighbors. Religion thus became another point of conflict. In the 18th century, about 10% of the population was Protestant, although this Protestant minority controlled much of Ireland's politics and economy.

Sometimes, however, the quest for Irish independence united Catholics and Protestants in common cause. In the late 18th century, a group of Catholic and Protestant Irish formed the United Irishmen, a group that was willing to battle for freedom. They fought to gain Irish independence, but like the others before them they were unsuccessful.

In 1800, Great Britain officially absorbed Ireland in the Act of Union. The English hoped that they would be able to establish a firmer hold over the island, however, their hopes remained unrealized as the Irish continued in their struggle.

In the 1840s the great potato famine struck the island, resulting in the deaths of close to a million people. At least two million more left Ireland, seeking refuge in other countries. Because potatoes were the primary source of food for at least 30% of the Irish, the blight was devastating and far-reaching. With the desperation bred on the instinct for survival, political conflict increased and violence and rebellions became common.

The road to independence, however, was a long one, the first step toward full autonomy for the Irish state coming after World War I with the Anglo-Irish Treaty of 1921 that provided dominion status to 26 counties in Ireland. While most of the Irish counties applauded their new status — won after years of strife — the six northeastern counties, because of a majority of Protestants in their population, retained close ties to England. These counties today make up Northern Ireland, which is yet administrated by England. Ireland finally achieved full independence in 1949 when the Republic of Ireland declared itself to be free. By this time, with the anguish of World War II still vivid in people's minds, and with England's colonial empire already well underway to dissolution, the English offered little protest.

Unfortunately, turmoil and conflict continued for years in Northern Ireland between Protestants and Catholics. Only since the mid-nineties has the violence declined, a direct result of the efforts of the region's leaders to find a peaceful solution to the tensions.

# Government

The Republic of Ireland has a parliamentary form of government, which consists of the president of the country and two houses. The legal framework for the government is embodied in a constitution adopted in 1937, referred to as the Bunreacht na hErieann. In most cases the laws written in the constitution may be changed only through a referendum of voters. Ireland's constitution is a strong one; its democracy is stable.

The Parliament is composed of two houses: the Dail, which is the lower chamber, and the Seanad, or Senate, the upper chamber. The Dail consists of 166 members, elected by the nation's voters, while the Seanad is composed of 60 members. Eleven of the Seanad's members are nominated by the prime minister and the other 49 are elected by delegates of the University of Dublin, and five panels of professional, trade, and cultural associations. Legislative authority is vested in the Dail and the Seanad.

Like the members of the Dail, the president is elected by citizens, 18 years of age and older. He or she is elected through direct vote for a term of seven years and may run for reelection only once. The president is a position in the government that wields little actual power. The most important act of the president is to appoint the prime minister, or taoiseach, who is the leader of the majority party in the Dail. The president also appoints judges to Ireland's courts.

The true executive of the government is the prime minister. After his appointment, the prime minister nominates ministers for the cabinet, who must be approved by the Dail. It is the duty of these individuals to help the prime minister in the governing of the country.

Ireland's judiciary is based on the system of common law that developed in the United Kingdom. The highest court is the supreme court, consisting of six judges. This court hears cases that focus on difficult legal questions and the constitutionality of Ireland's laws. The judiciary includes courts of criminal appeal, high courts, and circuit and district courts.

Ireland is divided into 26 counties, whose authority is further divided into numerous local county boards. Much of the administration of the country is carried out at the local level through county councils, borough corporations, urban councils, and town commissioners. Local administrators are typically elected by popular vote for five-year terms.

Through much of their history the Irish people fought for democracy. In large part because of this struggle modern Ireland is built on a firm constitution and respect for law and individual rights.

# Irish Tradition and Culture

Although Ireland's history can be traced to Neolithic times, its earliest inhabitants left little by which they can be remembered. Even the Celts, who we know much more about, left little of their civilization. With the establishment of the Catholic Church, however, the keeping of diligent records and a fine tradition of literature was begun.

Much of Ireland's early books are preserved at the University of Dublin in the Trinity College Library. Perhaps the greatest of these works is the *Book of Kells*, written in the 8th century, which is a copy of the Christian Gospels. This work is evidence for Christianity's dominance in Irish life. Featuring an artform known as illumination, the *Book of Kells* was created in ornate handwriting and contains exquisite illustrations highlighted with real gold. It is a marvelous, inspiring work, proof of the creative talent and learning that flourished in Ireland at a time much of Europe still languished in the Dark Ages.

Some historians argue that much of the Irish respect for literature evolved out of respect for the early Church's books and manuscripts, yet it is also likely that this respect grew out of the distant, misty past when Irish warriors listened in awe and admiration to sages and storytellers. In more modern times, the Irish have given the world some of its best literature through authors such as Jonathan Swift, Oscar Wilde, George Bernard Shaw, W.B. Yeats, James Joyce, and the Nobel Prize winner of 1995, Seamus Heaney. Such was the influence of Irish authors at the beginning of the 20th century that literary scholars refer to this time as the Irish Literary Revival.

Perhaps even more well known throughout the world than Irish literature is Irish music. The light and energetic tunes of Irish jigs, reels, and polkas are distinctive and have found their way into the music of other lands, particularly American folk and country music. The fiddle, accordion, flute, and bagpipe are some of the instruments common to Irish traditional music and are often heard at Irish celebrations. Along with other types of music, traditional Irish music may be heard at pubs, halls, and virtually any gathering of people at which musicians are present. Ireland is also known for its contemporary music. The rock group U2, for example, is popular throughout the world.

The Irish take great pride in their culture. Wherever they go, they keep and celebrate their customs and traditions. Just consider St. Patrick's Day Parades held to remember and honor the island's patron saint.

# Ireland — An Island for Everyone

People who visit Ireland for the first time are often surprised, and sometimes astonished, at the island's natural beauty and the warmth and friendliness of its people. Many of those familiar with the island feel that some of Ireland's most interesting and picturesque places may be found along and near its coasts. This is not to say that interior Ireland lacks interest; it is simply that the interior is comprised mostly of farmland crisscrossed by streams and accented with quiet lakes and quaint towns. It is near the coasts that most travelers and visitors find an assortment of things to do and places to see.

In Dublin, the capital, one may find activities and pursuits to satisfy virtually any need or desire. Although a major city, much of Dublin retains a small-town atmosphere. Its streets are clean and amazingly safe for a city of its size. Fine restaurants, night clubs, and hotels offer a variety of fare and entertainment, and countless shops carry an assortment of goods from local crafts to brand name products recognized worldwide.

Ireland's next largest city is Cork, situated above the River Lee. This is the site of Blarney Castle and the Blarney Stone. It is a popular spot for tourists who wish to kiss the Stone for good luck.

Galway is perhaps one of Ireland's most exciting towns, and in recent years has become a type of resort where people go to vacation or enjoy a day of leisure. Situated at the point where the River Corrib flows into Galway Bay, the city is built around the river, which meanders through its sections. In Galway is Eyre Square and the Church of St. Nicholas, the largest medieval church in Ireland.

Ireland's cities are not the only interesting places in the country. Many of its smaller towns and counties have plenty to offer visitors and tourists. Known for its mountains and lakes, County Mayo is an excellent vacation spot. County

Kerry is thought by some to be one of all Ireland's most beautiful places because of its mountains and countryside. Donegal Town is well known by those who wish to hike into rugged mountains or visit and hike about the inlets of Donegal Bay. Ennis, a town in County Clare, is site to a 13th-century monastery amid a plateau colored by wild flowers.

Unlike many other places around the world where the traveler would likely encounter rude crowds, traffic congestion, and crime, Ireland offers a lovely safe haven that contains numerous remarkable places to visit and explore.

## Opportunity in Ireland

During the last third of this century, Ireland has transformed itself into a wonderful site for investment. Since the 1960s, over a thousand overseas companies have come to Ireland and established businesses. Over the last 25 years the nation has developed an excellent atmosphere for business and investment, evolving to become one of the best locations for potential future growth in all of Europe.

The Irish government has actively pursued policies and programs that are designed to build and expand the nation's economy. Most importantly, the business climate has been made friendly and foreign investment has been encouraged. Entrepreneurs, investors, and companies that establish businesses in Ireland benefit from a variety of factors, including low corporate tax rates, a modern infrastructure, favorable investment environment, and tariff-free access to the markets of the Economic Union.

Along with the clear advantages it offers to businesses and investors, Ireland also offers much to those individuals who are in search of a new place to live that has a scenic environment and acceptable climate, as well a robust economy and a equitable tax system. Moreover, Ireland's people are warm and friendly, and its cities and towns enjoy low levels of crime. Whether for relocating to start a new career or business, or searching for a superior place to spend one's retirement, Ireland has something for everyone.

# Business in Ireland

Whether you wish to invest in Ireland in an existing business, open a branch office, or establish a new business in the country, Ireland offers significant advantages and incentives. The administration supports an environment that is both open and friendly to business, the result of which has been sustained impressive economic growth. It is noteworthy that the expanding economy has come in an era of low inflation.

Most economists expect Ireland's growth to remain strong and consistent, supported in part by accelerating growth in Europe and especially Britain. The vibrant economy in a climate of stable and low interest rates spurs consumer spending, capital investment in industry and commerce, and home construction. Each of these sectors in turn supports myriad economic activities which add to the country's overall growth. Along with domestic spending, substantial international investments continue to flow into the country, further strengthening the economy.

Unquestionably, Ireland offers major advantages to virtually any business, including:

- A modern business and industrial infrastructure.

- A young, educated, and skilled workforce. The workforce is English-speaking.

- Significant tax incentives, most important of which is a 10% corporate tax rate for many businesses until 2010. A similar tax rate applies for financial services until 2005. These rates are the lowest in Europe.

- A high-quality telecommunications system.

- A stable political climate where democracy and individual rights are respected.

- A business-friendly economic environment.

- Low costs for business.

- A stable currency.

- Low inflation.

- Duty-free access to the 370 million people who comprise the EU markets.

Few countries anywhere in the world can offer as many benefits to business as Ireland. The factors noted above clearly show Ireland as a potential site for significant and sustained economic expansion. The nation is emerging as one of the most impressive economies of Europe.

## The Change from an Agricultural to a Diversified Economy

In the past Ireland's economy was based largely on agriculture. Today, while still important, farm products account for only about 20% of the country's GNP. The change has come mostly through the development and growth of light industry, financial services, and tourism.

While the focus for future growth has been placed on specific industries and financial services, agriculture remains a vital part of the country's economy. Ireland's interior is home to countless fertile farms that produce potatoes, grain, fruits, vegetables, and sugar beets. Dairy products and cattle raising also account for a large share of the agricultural sector and add significantly to the country's exports. Ireland's cattle raising industry illustrates this well as the country is the largest net exporter of beef in the EU. Food and live animals account for 15% of the country's exports.

Exports are a particularly strong sector of Ireland's economy with about 80% of the country's GDP linked to exports. The EU is Ireland's most important trade partner with close to 70% of Irish exports sent to Europe annually. In recent years, however, Irish businessmen have sought to secure new markets throughout the world, and have fostered trade with the United States, Japan, and several other countries. Close to 10% of Ireland's food and animal trade, for example, is sent to countries of NAFTA. It is likely that Ireland's worldwide trade relations will expand as the nation grows into a global economy.

Ireland's impressive growth and its evolution from an economy based on almost entirely on agriculture to one firmly founded on industry, financial services, and tourism, as well as agricultural products, has been the result of sound government policies. Over the last several years, the Irish government has been consistent in formulating and enacting legislation that encourages foreign investment and industrial expansion. The government has developed numerous incentives that make Ireland a most attractive place for business.

Today Ireland has designated several sectors of the nation's economy as having high priority. These include:

- Financial services, including banking, mutual funds, and insurance.

- International services, including software development and support, multimedia, and teleservices.

- Electronics, including PC systems, semiconductors, and communications systems.

- Engineering, including automatives, aerospace, and industrial systems.

- Consumer products, including products for sports and leisure activities, personal care, and fashion.

- Healthcare, including pharmaceuticals, medical devices, and hospital products.

The government has also initiated programs designed to encourage and support food processing, textiles, brewing, and machinery for light industry. The country's growth has been impressive in that it has been sustained during a time inflation has been controlled. Because Irish firms have increased their efficiency and competitiveness — in part because of the country's expansion into world markets — Ireland's economy is expected to eventually pass the EU average.

Along with the strength of its many industries, Ireland has also emerged as a leading center for international offshore investments, and Dublin has become a center for the management of international funds in Europe. Dublin's International Financial Services Center (IFSC), established in 1987, focuses on funds management including such activities as international banking, insurance, asset finance, and corporate treasury.

The country's financial system is well up to the task of providing services for the nation's businesses, as well as international funds management. The financial system consists of various banks, investment and funds companies, and credit companies that provide consumers and businesses with the kinds of financial services that are available anywhere in the world. More than 30 major banks provide various services for their customers, from routine savings and checking accounts to sophisticated, global investment plans.

Ireland banks and investment houses offer many opportunities for investors. Since there are no exchange controls, there is no limit on the amount of money an individual can bring into Ireland. Individuals coming into the country and who wish to open bank or other financial accounts will most likely need to show a passport. If you wish to deposit or invest large sums of money, you may be asked to prove your identity. This is a result of the Criminal Justice Act, passed in 1994, which was enacted to prevent criminals from using Ireland as a site to launder money. Needing to show identification should not be taken as a sign of an overly zealous financial system; rather its purpose is to merely reduce the possibility of criminal activity. Upon settling in the country, you need only visit the offices of a reputable banker or financial house to obtain the necessary information regarding investments.

Not only is Ireland's financial system comprehensive, it is strong as well. Along with being responsible for issuing and protecting the value of the Irish pound, the nation's currency, the Central Bank of Ireland has the duty to supervise financial institutions and company.

## Incentives for Business and Investment

In an effort to maintain the forward momentum of the country's economy, the Irish government has enacted numerous significant incentives to encourage both domestic and foreign investment. Many of these incentives are fiscal and apply to companies whose operations include manufacturing, research and development, finance and services. These incentives have made Ireland an excellent place for both long- and short-term investment.

# Incentives for Manufacturing Companies

Major tax incentives are available for companies who manufacture products. (More information about the tax system in Ireland may be found in Chapter 3, "Ireland as a Tax Haven." The taxes noted here are limited to those associated with specific incentives for companies.) Manufacturing companies may be eligible to enjoy a corporate tax rate of 10%. Commonly known as "manufacturing relief," this rate is available to companies that carry on various operations, including the following:

- The manufacture of products for sale. The definition of "manufacture" is broad, including products which are normally considered manufactured, as well as those that are designated by law to qualify under this incentive. For example, computers — even though they are actually assembled rather than manufactured — qualify under the law.

- The processing of meat and fish, provided the processing is done in approved facilities.

- The providing or application of manufacturing services to the goods and products that belong to another company.

- The development of software that benefits from an employment grant from IDA Ireland. (The IDA is Ireland's Industrial Development Authority, which is detailed in an upcoming section.)

- Services engaged in data processing that benefit from an employment grant from IDA Ireland.

- Services of a technical or consultation nature, relating to software development or data processing that benefits from an employment grant from IDA Ireland.

- Operations focusing on the repairing or remanufacturing of computer equipment.

- Operations engaged in the repairing or maintaining of aircraft, their engines and parts.

- Enterprises related to the operation of ships in Ireland.

- Operations engaged in fish farming.

- Operations engaged in the cloning of plants.

- Operations related to the planning and design of engineering projects located beyond the EU.

- Operations such as special export houses that manage Irish manufactured products.

- Companies and individuals engaged in film-making in which 75% of the work for the film's production is conducted in Ireland. Companies that invest up to 1.05 million pounds and individuals who invest up to 25,000 pounds per annum qualify for tax relief on their investment.

The special 10% tax rate applies to both resident and non-resident companies that conduct their business in Ireland through a branch. Most companies can expect to enjoy the special rate until the year 2010. The exception here is export houses which may enjoy the special tax rate until 2000.

# Incentives for International Financial Services

The Irish government has not only enacted special legislation detailing incentives for manufacturing companies, but they have created important incentives for financial services companies that conduct their business in the Custom House Docks Area in Dublin. Companies that conduct their business in the following services are eligible for major incentives:

- Fund management.

- Banking services that are designed for working with foreign currencies.

- Operations that deal with bonds, equities, and futures in foreign currencies.

- Operations that deal with commodity futures or options.

- Insurance.

- Operations that provide processing, accounting, control, communication, and information storag e in the financial sector.

Companies that are engaged in the above operations may qualify for major incentives, including the following:

- A 10% tax rate on profits from certified activities. To be entitled to this rate a company must show that its business will add to the development of the area as an International Financial Services Center. A certificate must be obtained from the Minister of Finance.

- A 10-year exemption from local property taxes.

- For a 10-year period, a double deduction of the costs for rent in the center.

- Freedom of withholding tax in payment of interest to recipients.

- During the first year of operation, a write-off of 100% for expenditures for new equipment.

- During the first year of operation, a write-off of 100% for the costs of new facilities, including buildings, for owners who occupy their sites.

- During the first year of operation, a write-off of 54% for new building costs for lessors. In following years a write-off of the balance may be taken at 4% per annum.

The above incentives can be of significant advantage to international financial services companies, greatly adding to their competitiveness.

## Additional Business Incentives

The Irish government is quite serious in its encouragement and support of business. The administration rightly perceives that business growth directly translates to economic growth. As a result of this vision, the government has made additional incentives available to businesses, both domestic and foreign, in Ireland. Following are some of the most important:

- Foreign companies whose business is conducted through a branch in Ireland, or resident companies that have at least 90% of their issued share held by foreign interests are eligible to purchase tax free government securities.

- Companies that conduct and promote business in specific designated inner city areas in Dublin, Cork, Waterford, Galway, and Limerick are eligible for special urban renewal incentives.

- A variety of grants, particularly management development grants which help companies to recruit individuals with special skills, are available. Grants may total up to 50% of covered costs.

- The owner or owners of a stallion is not required to pay Irish tax on any income derived from stallion fees for the service of mares in Ireland. This is known as bloodstock tax incentives.

- Companies that manage woodlands are exempt from income tax and corporate tax under forestry tax incentives.

# The Shannon Airport Customs Free Zone

The Free Zone at Shannon Airport offer an opportunity for trading companies to take advantage of several incentives. Foreign or domestic companies that conduct their operations in the Free Zone, and contribute in some way to the development or use of Shannon Airport may be eligible for these incentives. Interested companies must apply for a license that will entitle them to a special tax incentive, which follows:

- Income derived from the company's Shannon Airport operations will be taxed at a rate of 10%. This special rate will continue through the end of December, 2005.

Various business operations will make a company eligible to benefit from the incentive, including:

- Offshore banking.

- Financial services.

- Insurance.

- Aircraft repair.

- Even the mere creation of jobs at the airport is often enough to enable a company to qualify for the tax incentive.

While all of these incentives certainly are evidence of the Irish government's commitment to business and economic growth, the government also provides services to businesses and industry through two agencies: Ireland's Industrial

Development Authority (IDA) and Forbairt. Between them, the two agencies provide services to both foreign and domestic firms. The needs of foreign firms is the focus of the IDA. The only exception is foreign companies whose primary business is food. Forbairt offers development and consultation services to domestic companies and companies whose main operations are food. Loan guarantees are made available under the Forbairt Enterprise Development Program to investors who are interested in obtaining financing for the establishment of a business in Ireland. Together, the two agencies provide expert help to companies in Ireland, helping them to realize all the advantages that Ireland offers to business.

Because it offers businesses and investors so many incentives, Ireland is among the most business-friendly countries in the world. More than a thousand international companies have established operations in Ireland during the past few decades, and many have continually expanded their business, committing more funds to investment. With a well-educated, English-speaking labor force, a modern, solid infrastructure, membership in and access to the markets of the EU, a government that is committed to supporting industry and financial services companies, Ireland unquestionably is a prime site for establishing a business, relocating an existing business, or starting a branch office.

# Ireland as a Tax Haven

The tax system in Ireland centers around individuals and corporations.  While its overall rates are not oppressive, the government nevertheless has enacted various legislation providing for numerous incentives and tax reductions.

Individuals are generally most concerned with income tax and tax on capital gains.  Income tax is payable at two rates:  27% and 48%; capital gains rates are 40%.  Most individuals are also obligated to pay social welfare levies of 7.25%.

An individual's residence and domicile determines whether or not he or she is subject to Irish taxes.  An individual is considered to be a resident of Ireland if he or she is present in the country for a period, or periods, totaling 183 days or more.  He or she will also be considered to be a resident if, in the year of assessment and the prior year of assessment, he or she was in the country in aggregate for 280 or more days.  If an individual who is not a resident wishes, he or she may apply for resident status.  The individual must satisfy the

Revenue Commissioners the he or she is in Ireland with the intention of being a resident in the upcoming year of assessment. For some individuals, Irish residency can indeed be advantageous in regard to taxes. However, no individual will be granted resident status in any year of assessment if he or she is not present in Ireland for at least a total of 30 days.

Domicile is associated with a person's permanent home. This in turn is usually defined as the "home to which he or she intends to return." For an individual to be considered as having an Irish domicile, he or she must set up a permanent residence in Ireland and give up his or her foreign home.

Irish residents, non-residents, non-resident individuals who are normally residents, and others, such as estates of the deceased, are generally liable for Irish taxes under the following categories:

- Residents — worldwide income; some sources may be exempt.

- Non-domiciled residents — Irish income and income from the United Kingdom, and also foreign income remitted to Ireland.

- Non-resident individuals who are normally residents — foreign investment income and income from Irish sources. Exempt is income from trading, professional, and employment derived from duties performed abroad.

- Non-resident and those not normally resident individuals — Irish source income only, which may be exempt or reduced because of tax treaties.

Income from various sources is liable for tax, including the follow major categories:

- Income from employment, directorships, etc.

- Business profits.

- Dividends and other distributions from Irish companies that are considered to be resident.

- Income from interest, including that derived from Irish government securities, deposits with banks, and other financial institutions.

- Income from sources abroad.

- Income from real estate in Ireland.

- Other incomes that are not included above.

It should be noted that various personal allowances are permitted under the tax code, which reduce the amount of tax many individuals pay. This is especially true for individuals over 65 years of age. Rent and mortgage relief allowances are also available, as are capital gains personal exemptions.

Following is a list highlighting some of the most common allowances permitted individuals under the Irish tax system. Note that all amounts are in Irish pounds.

```
Personal Allowances
Single Person          2,650
Married Person         5,300
Widowed Person         3,150
Widowed Person (in year of bereave-
ment)                  5,300
One-Parent Family Allowances
Widowed Person         2,150
Other                  2,650
Widowed Parent Allowance
Determined by when bereaved —
500 to 1,500
```

Age Allowance

Single                      200

Married                     400

Blind Allowance

Individual                  700

Both Spouses Blind        1,600

Care of Incapacitated Person

7,500 (maximum)

Care of Incapacitated Child

700 (maximum)

Care of Dependent Relative

110

In general, residents and those individuals domiciled in Ireland are required to pay taxes on their income and gains derived from around the world. Residents who are not domiciled in Ireland are required to pay Irish tax on income obtained from Irish and United Kingdom sources. They are required to pay tax on income obtained from other sources only in cases that it is remitted to Ireland. Special tax categories exist for investments such as bank deposits, equity investments, and life assurance, the tax in many cases being 10%.

Corporate taxes are based on a company's income and capital gains. Resident companies — those whose central management exercises control of the company in Ireland — are required to pay tax on income they obtain from around the world. Non-resident companies are obligated to pay tax only on income derived from their business in Ireland, including income that is in some way connected to Irish sources. The standard rate of corporation tax in Ireland was reduced from 38% to 36% on April 1, 1997. On the same day .the reduced corporate tax rate was decreased from 30% to 28%. In addition, many businesses qualify for the 10% rate under special incentives designed for manufacturing and financial service companies. (See Chapter 2, "Business in Ireland.")

As with individuals, the resident status of companies determines in large part their liability to pay Irish taxes. The determining factor is the site of the company's central management, usually the place where the company's board of directors meet. Quite simply, a company whose central management is located in Ireland is treated as a resident company. Companies whose central management is not located in Ireland are treated as non-resident.

Resident companies are liable to Irish tax as follows:

- Corporation tax on worldwide profits.

- Resident companies are not liable to income tax, or generally to capital gains tax.

Non-resident companies are liable to Irish corporation tax only as follows:

- Its trading income arises from the branch or agency.

- Income from property or rights held or used by the branch or agency.

- Capital gains from the disposal of any Irish assets.

- Income tax on income gained from other Irish sources.

It should be noted that a variety of exemptions, deductions, and reductions are available depending on the individual company's business and operations. For example, financial services companies enjoy various benefits under the existing tax laws. (See Chapter 4, "Ireland as a Tax Haven.")

# Collection of Irish Taxes

Irish taxes are collected in one of two ways: by deduction at the source of the income or self-assessment. Three major types of taxes collected at source include:

- The Deposit Interest Retention Tax (DIRT). This tax is applied to interest paid by most institutions that offer deposits, such as banks.

- A payroll deduction tax, commonly called "pay as you earn" or (PAYE).

- A social security payroll tax, referred to as pay-related social insurance (PRSI).

The self-assessment part of the system requires individuals and companies to make timely returns regarding their income. Failure to do so results in penalties and interest charges. Along with income, other taxes, including VAT, inheritance taxes, gift taxes, and residential property taxes are paid according to the self-assessment schedule.

For companies, the schedule requires them to make a return based on their income within nine months of the end of each accounting period. Within six months of the end of the accounting period they are required to pay at lest 90% of the final tax due in regard to that period.

For individuals, the schedule requires them to complete and file an annual return based on their income on January 31 following the end of each tax year. The tax year in Ireland ends on April 5. Those individuals who have income that is not subject to tax being deducted at source are required to make a tax payment equal to at least 90% of their total tax liability on November 1 of each tax year. A qualified Irish accountant can help individuals and companies who are new to Ireland comply with the various laws and regulations.

# Value Added Tax (VAT)

Ireland also has a Value Added Tax (VAT) for which the standard rate is 21%. Reduced rates are included in the tax code at 12.5%, 2.5%, and 0% for certain goods and services.

With some exceptions, VAT is charged on the value of goods and services supplied in Ireland. To incur VAT on these goods and services, they must be supplied in Ireland by an individual who is subject to tax in the course of his or her business. Products imported from outside the EU are also subject to VAT. A variety of goods and services, which includes those identified as export sales, are not subject to VAT. Various exemptions and deferments are also possible.

For goods imported from outside the EU, VAT is payable at the point of entry. However, a company that manufactures products and exports out of the EU at least 75% in value of the products it produces is allowed to import materials and components required for the finished products without being subject to VAT.

## Double Taxation Treaties

Countries sign double taxation treaties to eliminate double taxation. Double taxation agreements benefit taxpayers who derive income from both states, which in the absence of the treaty would both tax the individual. Under a double taxation treaty, states usually agree to make allowances that ease the burden of tax on the individual. Depending on the state of residence, income might be exempted by one of the states, or credit might be given for tax that is paid. The result is that the taxpayer pays less.

Double taxation treaties also serve the interests of the states by promoting trade and economic activity that might otherwise be curtailed under the burden of double taxation. In an effort to expand its worldwide trade, Ireland has entered into double taxation treaties with 28 countries. Negotiations with other countries is on-going. Ireland has signed double taxation treaties with the following countries:

| | |
|---|---|
| Australia | Republic of Korea |
| Austria | Luxembourg |
| Belgium | Netherlands |
| Canada | New Zealand |
| Czech Republic | Norway |
| Cyprus | Pakistan |
| Denmark | Portugal |
| Finland | Poland |
| France | Russia |
| Germany | Spain |
| Hungary | Sweden |
| Italy | Switzerland |
| Israel | United Kingdom |
| Japan | United States |

# Taxes and Investments

Without question, Ireland offers many tax incentives for businesses. Most people don't realize that Ireland also offers various investment opportunities for individuals that are tax-free or are taxed at low rates. Following are some of the best.

- Ireland's postal service. *An Post* offers accounts that generate tax-free income. *An Post* Savings Certificates are tax-free and privacy is assured. Individuals may invest up to 60,000 pounds at an interest rate of up to 40% on maturity, which is five years, nine months. Interest is compounded every six months. If necessary, you can obtain your cash in seven days. *An Post* also offers savings bonds and National Installment Savings. Savings bonds pay close to 20% interest for a period of three years. National Installment Savings have an interest rate of close to 50%, which is paid over six years.

- Bank accounts for non-residents. The major banks in Ireland offer various accounts and bonds designed for non-residents. Privacy is assured, there are no maximum amounts to investment, and there are no Irish taxes. Interest rates vary, depending on the specific investment.

- Business Expansion Schemes are tax-relief investments offered through government companies. They are designed for taxpayers who have high incomes, but can help individuals reduce their tax burden substantially. Investments in films is one of the more popular enterprises that falls within the Business Expansion Schemes. Be cautious with these investments, however, because the risk with some may be high. Be sure to obtain sound financial advice before committing funds to any investment in this category.

Compared to many countries, Ireland's tax system is not onerous. While all sources of income are included, there are also various deductions and allowances that lessen the tax burden for most payers. Specific incentives and deductions that bestow upon Ireland the mantel of one of the world's prime "tax havens" are detailed in the upcoming chapter.

# Establishing a Non-resident Company in Ireland

An Irish company that enjoys non-resident status is a company that is incorporated in the Republic of Ireland and is subject to Irish law, but is not subject to Irish taxation because it is not a resident company. Significant tax benefits, however, are not the only advantages to the establishment of an Irish non-resident company. All Irish companies benefit from a stable, democratic political system, Ireland's membership in the European Union, a superior infrastructure, English as an international language, and an educated workforce.

In recent years Ireland has emerged as a prime location from which to operate offshore businesses. A modern state with easy access to Europe's markets, Ireland is the country of choice for many who consider the establishment of a new company. Irish law permits non-resident companies to engage in a variety of businesses without burdensome restrictions and requirements. Some common business operations include:

> \* Companies that hold financial or commercial titles, which may include bank accounts, trusts, investment plans, and fixed deposits.
>
> \* Companies engaged in international trade.
>
> \* Companies whose business includes marketing or promotional activities.
>
> \* Companies that own materials and/or property. This includes intellectual properties.
>
> \* Companies that own shares of other companies.

Based on the definitions above, it is clear that countless enterprises make companies eligible for non-resident status. Of course there are some requirements that companies must meet to be considered non-resident, but these are relatively minor and are easy to satisfy.

For a company to be deemed non-resident, the central control must be exercised from outside of Ireland. Furthermore, the company may not trade in Ireland or through an agency or organization in Ireland. Finally, the company may not have any income or gains arising in Ireland.

Under the 1986 Irish Companies Act, all Irish companies are required to maintain a registered office, have at least two directors and two shareholders, prepare annual reports, and undergo auditing. Moreover, the accounts must be approved in an annual general meeting and filed each year.

In addition to the above, there are some corporate considerations that must be taken into account. These include:

* There must be a public registry of shareholders.

* While the company must have at least two directors, no corporate directors are permitted. There must be public registry of directors. The company's officers need not reside in Ireland; they may be residents of other countries.

* The company must appoint a secretary.

It is also noteworthy that there is no minimum requirement for capital, and the share capital may be in any currency. However bearer shares are not allowed.

Incorporating a company in Ireland is rather easy in comparison to many places around the world. Often it requires less than a day for papers to be filed and for a name to be approved. In most cases, a company can receive all of its documentation and be incorporated in less than two weeks.

Numerous tax benefits are available to Irish non-resident companies. The most important of these include:

* No Irish tax on income.

* No Irish capital gains tax.

* No Irish withholding taxes assessed on payments of dividends, interest or royalties.

Irish non-resident companies clearly enjoy an enormous tax advantage when compared to the tax burdens of companies in other jurisdictions. For individuals who are considering options by which they may limit the tax liabilities of their current business, or those who are considering starting a new business with minimal tax exposure, an Irish non-resident company may be the answer.

Although incorporating a company in a new land may seem daunting to some, the establishment of an Irish non-resident company is quite simple. Virtually any law or accounting firm in Ireland can provide you with the details you need to get started. To find such firms, you may contact the Irish Development Authority (IDA). Of course, the IDA also provides development and consultation services to all overseas companies, except those companies whose business operations focus on food. For the address and phone numbers of an IDA office in your area, see the Appendix at the end of this book.

The value of establishing a non-resident company in Ireland cannot be understated. Not only does the company enjoy generous tax advantages, few restrictions are placed on the company's business activities.

# The Globalization of Ireland's Economy: Opportunities for You

One of the most significant developments for Ireland during the 1990s has been the emergence of a global economy. Without question, today Ireland's business ties reach around the world. Not only has the country become a major financial center, it has become a site of high growth for countless businesses, resulting in impressive returns for investors.

Since the early 1970s, Ireland has transformed itself from primarily an agriculture-based economy to a diversified, technological-based economy. Whereas about 20% of Ireland's exports were manufactured goods some 30 years ago, such products now account for about 70% of the nation's exports. Indeed in many sectors exports have been the driving force behind growth. Between 1994 and 1996, for example, Ireland's export growth rate was the highest in the EU. During the same years the nation's overall economy grew at an average rate of more than 7%. Just as impressively, between 1992 and 1996, the country experienced an inflation rate of a mere 2.2%.

Sectors    including    electronics,    software, telecommunications, pharmaceuticals, aviation, automotives, construction, and consumer products are growing domestically as well as gaining new markets throughout the EU and the world at large. Although the EU remains Ireland's biggest trading partner — Irish firms have doubled their market share in Europe since 1980 — close to 30% of all Irish exports are sold outside of the EU with about 20% sent to markets around the world other than those in North America.

Irish companies have benefited greatly from the overall expansion in world trade. As more countries around the world acquire and develop better technology, their ability to trade improves. This is reflected in the fact that since 1990 world trade has grown by 6% annually, an increase of 50% over the rate of growth in the 1980s. It should be noted that Irish companies have tended to grow faster than the general rate of world trade, which helps account for Ireland's surging economy.

Several factors support and encourage this growth. Clearly, the liberalization of trade regulations, the explosion in information, the rapid development of advanced communications systems, and pent-up demand of consumers from many developing countries are keys to Ireland's global economic expansion. But there is more. Ireland enjoys a unique position in that it benefits from the increase of world trade, yet also gains great advantage from its membership in the European Union. The EU constitutes an enormous market of 370 million consumers. Its GDP is $8.8 billion, and it is pressing ahead with plans to embrace a standard monetary unit. Just as importantly, the EU is looking eastward toward the growing economies of Eastern Europe, some, if not most, of which are expected to seek membership in the union. This will expand the consumer base of the EU, adding immense new markets.

Irish companies also expect to benefit from other trade groups. In the Americas, NAFTA includes the U.S., Canada, and Mexico, while Mercosur includes Brazil, Argentina, Paraguay and Uruguay. Asia also offers new markets. The Asia-Pacific Economic Cooperation Forum (APEC) represents nearly half of the earth's entire population and close to 40% of global trade. In addition to this, the ASEAN countries of Singapore, Malaysia, Indonesia, Thailand, the Philippines, Brunei, and Vietnam present major markets. Although India and China have been slower than some of their neighbors to join the global marketplace, in recent years they have moved forward to build trade with companies throughout the world. These various trading groups present massive potential markets for the products of Irish firms, which have gained vital experience during the last decade in establishing trade relations with countries the world over. That experience is likely to give many Irish companies the competitive edge to secure new markets before their rivals.

It is obvious that the world is evolving into a marketplace where all companies have the opportunity to sell their products and services. However, the greatest success will come to those companies that enjoy the advantages of a supportive business environment as Irish companies do.

Ireland's expanding economy offers unique and exciting opportunities to investors and entrepreneurs. While companies and industries in countless businesses throughout the nation are taking advantage of these opportunities, several important sectors stand out. These sectors include:

- Aerospace and Related Industries.

- Agriculture.

- Automotives.

- Clothing and Textiles.

- Consumer Products.

- Electronics.

- Engineering Services.

- Pharmaceuticals.

- Print and Packaging Services.

- Process Control Services.

- Software Development.

- Telecommunications.

In the upcoming pages these sectors will be examined in detail. Ireland's steadily growing economy offers countless opportunities for investors.

# Opportunities in Aerospace and Related Industries

Having long been a prime destination for the world's airlines, Ireland has become an important center for the aerospace industry. Numerous major airlines rely on Ireland as a base for their operations, including: Air France, Alitalia,

British Airways, China Airlines, Iberia, Japan Airlines, Lufthansa, Saudi Arabian Airlines, Singapore Airlines, and Swissair.

Although the main focus of the aerospace industry remains keyed to the commercial jet market and repair and maintenance of engines and airframes, numerous related industries are growing just as fast. The services of companies and individuals who can provide expertise in a variety of areas are almost always in high demand. These include services that:

- Maintain and repair aircraft.

- Manufacture aircraft parts and components.

- Recruit and train personnel for the aerospace industry.

- Offer consulting services that can improve the efficiency of aerospace firms.

- Develop and provide software necessary for aircraft and airports.

- Provide telecommunications equipment.

- Offer financial services.

- Offer programs and products for space-related operations.

Individuals or companies that can offer any of the above services will likely have ready customers in Ireland. Likewise, investors who are interested in a sector that has potential for high-growth might consider aerospace companies as well as those in related areas.

# Opportunities in Agriculture

Although Ireland's economy has diversified, agriculture, the nation's traditional economy, is still vital and offers many opportunities for investors. Indeed, the quality of Ireland's agricultural products is prized, particularly throughout the EU.

Over the years Ireland's agricultural machinery and equipment producers have developed quality products that have proven invaluable to Irish farmers as well as farmers throughout the world. Irish agricultural products range from products that ensure healthy grass to heavy duty plows and harvesters. Because agriculture remains essential to Ireland's overall economy, opportunities for investors and entrepreneurs are plentiful, including:

- The production of agricultural equipment.

- Consulting services for agricultural management.

- Marketing expertise, particularly in the establishment of new trade contacts.

- The development of new products.

While most people think of traditional farms when they consider the agricultural sector, the definition of farming is rather broad in Ireland. In recent years the agricultural sector has come to include forestry, aquaculture, and stud farms.

A particular opportunity exists in forestry. In the past, because its climate is well suited for trees, Ireland was almost completely forested. With the world's demand for lumber and wood products exceeding supply (and likely to continue to do so over the long term), and with generous grants, establishing a forestry company could result in handsome profits.

Both residents and non-residents can invest in forestry companies, which enjoy special consideration from the state-owned Forestry Board. Banks and other financial institutions also support forestry enterprises, often providing financing at relatively modest terms. Perhaps most importantly, however, is that profits from forestry are exempt from Irish tax.

Yet another potential area of investment is aquaculture. Although lobsters and mussels are important aquaculture products, most Irish aquaculture is based on oysters. Oyster farmers typically conduct their business on waters owned by the Department of Marine, paying the department a fee for usage. However, generous grants are available to set up an aquaculture business, which because of the popularity of oysters, can be quite profitable.

Establishing and maintaining a stud farm is potentially one of the most profitable uses of land in Ireland. With the goal to develop a non-thoroughbred horse industry, the government offers various grants designed to encourage the breeding of quality horses, and exempts any profits received from stud services from Irish taxes.

Of course, rather than establishing a major business, some people might simply prefer to buy an Irish farm because of the bucolic life it offers. Clearly, Ireland's agriculture sector offers numerous opportunities for investment.

# Opportunities in Automotives

Ireland's automotive component industry is a strong one. About 50% of the country's automotive companies are Irish owned, with much of the remainder subsidiaries of companies based in the U.S. and Germany. Some of these companies include Ford, BMW/Rover, Fiat, Mercedes, GM/Opel, Volvo, and VW/Audi. This sector focuses virtually all of its production for the export market, with most of the products being sent to Europe.

The companies in this sector are solid and competitive, and rely on numerous related companies to support their production. Just some areas of opportunity include:

- Alarm systems.

- Automotive wiring.

- Consulting services.

- Electrochemical relays.

- Electronics.

- Marketing analysis.

- Expertise in technical systems related to automotive parts.

- Expertise in the development of rubber products.

- Expertise in meeting the needs of international customers.

Because the market for automotive products around the world is expected to grow — particularly in developing countries — it is expected that Ireland's automotive component sector will thrive in the coming years.

# Opportunities in Clothing and Textiles

Ireland's long-established tradition in wool and linens is known worldwide. Many companies — including Dunhill, Harrods, Hesse Mail Order, Marks & Spencer, Mitsukoshi, Nordstroms, Macy's, and Saks 5th Avenue — are customers for Irish clothing products. In recent years Ireland's clothing sector has been enhanced through the eye-catching creations of Irish clothing designers.

Irish clothing manufacturers are active in the full spectrum of apparel, including clothing for men, women, and children. They produce clothing for all seasons and just about every occasion.

Because the clothing industry is well established, opportunities exist in its potential expansion. Individuals, entrepreneurs, and investors might look for areas in marketing, contract manufacturing, mail order company supply, and international marketing as prime areas of opportunity.

Based on the past success of this sector, it is likely that Irish clothing manufacturers will continue to be an important part of the Irish economy.

# Opportunities in Consumer Products

During the past few decades Irish manufacturers of consumer products have become world leaders. The quality of Irish products is high, and their reputation is well established. Many Irish companies ship their products to major stores throughout Europe and the U.S. Moreover, they are constantly expanding their markets, making this sector truly global in scope.

Just some categories of consumer products in which Irish companies excel include:

- Crystal.

- Jewelry.

- Ceramics.

- China.

- Tableware.

- Cutlery.

- Toys and games.

- Sporting goods.

- Stationery and paper products.

- Hardware products.

- Furniture.

- Clothing (see previous section).

- Floor coverings.

- Garden products.

Individuals and companies that can provide services that support the manufacturers of consumer products will find various opportunities from which they might profit. Consumer products is an extremely competitive sector and Irish companies, like other companies, are always in search of a competitive edge.

# Opportunities in Electronics

Over the past several years, Ireland's electronics sector has been one of the economy's strongest. Irish-owned companies and multinational corporations comprise the bulk of this sector, providing electronic equipment to a varied customer base including: Daimler Benz, Apple, IBM, Dell, Gateway 2000, Nokia, Compaq, Philips, Siemens, and Ericsson.

The companies of this sector offer many different products, including:

- Parts and components for telecommunications equipment.

- Equipment for information technologies.

- Parts for consumer electronics.

- Components for computers.

- Parts, components, and equipment for the automotive industry.

- Equipment for medical devices.

Opportunities abound in industries that supports producers or sellers of electronics. While some of these, of course, are state-of-the-art design, others are of a rather less exotic nature but still potentially profitable. Operations that support the electronics sector include companies whose primary business might be in circuit boards, converters, cables, connectors, terminators, tapes, metal parts, precision metal assemblies, PCB substrates, and plastics.

# Opportunities in Pharmaceuticals

Of the world's 15 leading pharmaceutical companies, 12 have plants in Ireland, making this sector a dynamic force in the marketplace. The pharmaceutical sector is comprised of both domestic and multinational corporations that are engaged in a wide assortment of products and services, from basic research and development to production and distribution. Merck Sharpe, Pfizer, Rhone Poulenc, Sandoz, Schering Plough, and Smithline Beecham are just some of the top companies that are a part of this sector.

Because of its strong and expanding presence in the marketplace, Ireland's pharmaceutical sector offers opportunity for investors who wish to buy into an established company, as well as those who are interested in starting a company. Opportunities abound for companies that offer marketing, consultation, and financial services geared to pharmaceutical companies, research and development, and testing and clinical trials.

# Opportunities in Print and Packaging Services

Most companies rely, at least to some degree, on companies that offer print and/or packaging services. Riding the crest of Ireland's overall economic expansion throughout the late 1980s and 1990s has been the print and packaging services sector. While this sector has worked to meet the needs of Ireland's various businesses, some of its greatest growth has been a result of rapidly expanding sectors such as computer hardware and software, pharmaceuticals, electronics, and consumer goods.

The print and packaging sector is quite broad, including such activities and services as:

- Production of printed materials with state-of-the-art quality.

- Production of cartons, labels, and enclosures.

- Production of discs.

- Replication of discs.

- Printing of technical support services.

- Management of data.

With the demand for such services likely to continue to rise in upcoming years, it is almost certain that long-term growth will be assured. Clearly any business that is a part of this sector, or can support enterprises of this sector, will enjoy excellent prospects for profitability.

## Opportunities in Process Control Services

Companies throughout the world require various services in automation and instrumentation. Ireland's process control sector provides services to companies worldwide, including such leaders as Intel, Siemens, Texas Instruments, AT&T, NEC, Dell, Compaq, Fuji, Toshiba, Ericsson, and Rolls Royce.

Irish companies of this sector have developed superior services in the following:

- Automation systems.
- Motor technology.
- Computers.
- Telecommunications.
- Robotics.
- Semi-conductors.
- Power generating systems.
- Machine tools.
- Aerospace.
- Food processing.
- Oil and gas.
- Petrochemicals.
- Plastics.
- Pharmaceuticals.

Because the companies that provide process control services have such a large client base — their customers are found in virtually every major economic sector — numerous opportunities exist for entrepreneurs and investors.

## Opportunities in Software

Ireland's emergence as a software development and exporter has been truly impressive. Only the U.S. develops and exports more software than Ireland. Most of the world's leading software companies — including Microsoft, Oracle, IBM, Digital, and Claris — have a presence in Ireland, where they are taking advantage of the country's high level of technological expertise, its young and dynamic workforce, and the support of numerous telecommunications and high-tech companies.

Over 400 Irish software companies compete in world markets, where their reputation for quality, sophistication, and creativity are well known and respected. Indeed many of these companies are rapidly becoming world leaders in their areas of expertise.

Countless opportunities are available in this sector, including:

- The need for individuals with advanced technological skills.

- The need for individuals with computer-based skills.

- The need for innovative products that are at the forefront of the fast-changing and expanding field of electronics and computers.

- The need for individuals with marketing skills that will enable companies to tap into the exploding markets of the internet.

- The need for individuals and companies that can develop and deliver cutting edge software products.

- The need for individuals and companies that can expand this sector's importance into other areas.

With the growth of technology and increased use of computers and software assured by an expanding global marketplace, there is no apparent limit to the potential of Ireland's software sector.

# Opportunities in Telecommunications

With the demand for greater communications, Ireland's telecommunications sector is enjoying exceptional and prolonged growth. This growth is likely to continue.

Major companies such as At&T, Motorola, and Ericsson have established operations in the country, and with their expertise and global experience have helped to make telecommunications a significant export.

Irish companies benefit from a modern, high-quality telecommunications infrastructure, which supports both domestic and global expansion. These companies are some of the leaders in their fields and present investors, entrepreneurs, and individuals with an astonishing array of opportunities, including:

- The need for individuals and companies with marketing expertise.

- The need for individuals and companies who can provide management services required by the telecommunications sector.

- The need for individuals and companies that can provide software expertise and services.

- The need for individuals and companies that can develop new technologies and products that can exploit the growing field of telecommunications.

During the past several years Ireland has positioned itself to be at the front of the Information Age. To a great extent the success of companies today depends on their ability to communicate and manage information. This is why Ireland's telecommunications sector is likely to enjoy robust growth for quite some time.

From its agricultural economy Ireland has developed into a high-tech land of vitality and energy. In its business-friendly climate, Irish companies are given the encouragement they need to become innovative and competitive, and are well able to match their products and services against those of the best companies from around the world.

# Moving to Ireland

If you are considering moving to Ireland, but are worried about the cost of housing, you will likely be quite pleased with the information you will find in this chapter. Housing in Ireland is reasonably priced, and the housing market is stable. Whether you are looking for a permanent home, a vacation home, or property simply for investment, Ireland undoubtedly has something to fit your budget and tastes. For between $10,000 and $20,000 American dollars, you can purchase a small home in Ireland. Prices increase with size, of course, but the prices of homes in Ireland seldom approach housing costs common in other advanced nations. Cozy cottages with thatched roofs, large sprawling homes surrounded by acres of lovely meadows, even castles that have guarded the Irish countryside for hundreds of years are on the market.

Like any housing market in any part of the world, the prices of property rise and fall depending on location. Generally, prices are higher the closer you are to Dublin. Nice homes in the capital usually sell for a premium. Conversely, homes in isolated areas, far from major towns or cities are often least expensive. However, there are many fine locations in Ireland where beautiful properties can be bought for prices that most newcomers from other countries of the industrial world would consider true bargains.

Following are descriptions of some areas that newcomers might consider for purchasing property:

- Dublin — A fine site if you like a city atmosphere. Prices are higher than most other parts of the country, but Dublin is clean, safe, and quite picturesque. It offers all of the advantages that big cities anywhere else may offer, but without the crime, pollution, and congestion. Dublin is both cosmopolitan and quaint.

- The Southeast: Kildare, Wicklow, Carlow, Kilkenny, and Waterford — One of the sunniest regions of Ireland, property prices fall within the median. The general landscape is one of gently rolling hills that are highlighted by excellent farmlands. This area is close to Britain, if travel to England is desired.

- Cork and Kerry — At the southernmost part of Ireland, Cork and Kerry offer both gentle country and dramatic headlands that push out into the Atlantic. Delightful, quiet fishing villages are found along the coast. The region is unspoiled and its people are warm and friendly. The prices of homes are very reasonable.

- Limerick — Connected to the Atlantic by the Shannon River, Limerick is one of Ireland's most well known cities. While Limerick is certainly a worthy place to consider living, it is surrounded by many charming villages and towns, including Adare, Cashel, and Killaloe. The scenery throughout the area includes lush farmlands, scenic glens, and low Home prices, particularly in some of the smaller towns, are very modest.

- Galway — Dominating western Ireland, Galway is an energetic city. A choice of many newcomers and a center for tourism, the prices of homes tend to be higher than Ireland's average. However, the towns throughout the region often contain better prices. Overall, the region is rural and relatively empty compared to some other parts of Ireland. Beautiful countryside interspersed with mountains and bogs make this region the first choice for many newcomers.

- Mayo and Sligo — A wondrous landscape, high cliffs, breathtaking eaches, and reasonable prices make this region of the northwest a fine place to live. While much of Sligo's rugged charm is found inland, Mayo is admired for its marvelous coastline. Prices of homes here are reasonable.

- Donegal — An excellent choices if you like spectacular coastlines and proximity to mountains. The prices of homes in Donegal are quite reasonable, and the area is not nearly as populated as Galway or Dublin.

- Interior Ireland: Cavan, Louth, Longford, Meath, Westmeath, and Offaly — Many of Ireland's visitors ignore the interior, believing that more wonders may be found along Ireland's coasts. To some extent this is true — for tourists. But for those who are seeking to relocate to Ireland, the interior offers some of the best prices for homes, as well as quiet, pretty pastures, lakes, and marshes. For many people who wish to relocate to Ireland, the interior should be a prime consideration.

## Finding the Home of Your Dreams

Locating a home to buy in Ireland is much like buying a home anywhere else, with some notable differences. Most importantly, since you are moving to Ireland from another country, you must familiarize yourself with the various regions of Ireland so that you are able to make a good decision regarding which region would be most agreeable to you. This cannot be understated. Before buying a home in Ireland, it is vital that you visit the country for a sufficiently long enough time — perhaps several visits — so that you may travel through the country's different regions and acquaint yourself with them.

This doesn't mean a cursory drive-through. You should visit many locations and explore them thoroughly. Even though you might initially feel that you'd like to live in a small village, visit villages as well as towns and cities. You might find that a bigger town, or maybe even a city like Dublin, is more to your liking. Eat in local restaurants, talk with business owners and residents, and explore the area. Note the terrain, the types of entertainment and recreation available, the availability of services such as communications, healthcare, and utilities. Write down notes if you find that helpful, listing different places and the things you like and dislike about each one. Perhaps create a chart which will make it easier for you to compare and contrast different places. When you speak with people, ask about the climate, the local government, and whether they like living in the region. Encourage them to be open and honest with their answers. If many say they would move if they could, you might want to rethink this place as a potential home. Whenever you are evaluating a place, remember that the more specific your questions, the more keen your eye, and the more discriminate your observation, the more likely you will uncover information that will help you determine if the place is one in which you'd like to live.

When considering a potential home, be sure to take into account all of your family's members. If a family member is not comfortable with a place, it may not be a wise selection. In the end, a new home that is not satisfying to all those involved will likely lead to resentment and strife.

After having visited various regions and towns in Ireland, create a short list of possible places you'd like to live. Visit them again. At this point you might like to enlist the services of Irish real estate agents, who are easy to locate through local phone books. The internet is also a potential source under "Ireland, real estate," and similar search terms.

When dealing with any agent, be sure that you remain in control of which properties you'd like to see and also any negotiations. Avoid being pressured. If you become uncomfortable, step back and reevaluate your situation. Take your time. Buying property in another country requires caution and clear-thinking. Avoid making an offer on the first day you visit a property. Things sometimes look differently in the morning.

When you become interested in a home, it is the time to ask a variety of questions, including:

- What is the asking price? What is the price the owners will settle for? (This may be hard to obtain until the negotiations have proceeded, but it is worthwhile to ask. Sometimes agents will reveal that the owner will accept a much lower price.) Be alert to hints that the owners might be in a hurry to sell.

- What are the taxes you will need to pay?

- Are there possible repairs? Be sure to check the house carefully. A thatch-roofed cottage may appear quaint, but the roof might leak. For some houses, especially older ones, you might be required to renovate them and bring them up to modern codes. It is better to find this out before you buy than after. Some older homes or manors might need utilities to be modernized. Such things can escalate your costs rapidly.

- Ask about any hidden costs you might encounter, carefully noting the real estate agent's response. Many real estate agents will answer all of your questions honestly, however, for those that might not, you might learn just as much from the way they avoid or try to speak around your question.

- If you intend to arrange financing, ask for contacts with bankers. Before agreeing to any deal, you may wish to contact bankers yourself and go over details regarding financing.

The tone of these questions is not meant to imply that buying a home in Ireland is risky, however, whenever buying property, prudence is necessary, particularly when buying in a country other than one's birth. Securing the services of a reputable attorney and real estate agent can, of course, help to ensure that the home you buy will be everything you expect it to be.

Ultimately, buying a home in Ireland may be reduced to the well-known adage: "Buyer beware." Before making any purchase, be sure you have found out everything you need to know about the property, and proceed only when you are certain it is the right property for you.

## Living in Ireland — What to Expect

Along with being aware of general information about Ireland, you will need to know requirements and regulations that will affect your move to the country. Most importantly, if you plan to reside in Ireland for more than three months, you will be required to obtain a Certificate of Registration, which you may obtain at the local police (or Garda) station. To acquire the certificate, you will be expected to show all documents related to your entering the country, including passport, work permits, and passport photographs. Children under the age of 16 do not have to register; children 16 or older must. If, after you have registered, you decide to move to a new location in Ireland, you must advise Aliens Registration or your local police station before you move, and then report to your new local police station after you have moved.

Acquiring Irish citizenship is relatively easy. There are four methods by which to do so: being born in Ireland, marrying an Irish citizen, naturalization, and having descended from an Irish citizen. For more information about citizenship, see Chapter 7.

Following are a number of items you will need to know about living in Ireland:

- Driver's license — If you have a valid American driver's license, you may use it for one year after you have arrived in Ireland. If you have a valid license from an EC country, you may visit the Motor Taxation Office and obtain an Irish license. Individuals from other countries may need to apply for an Irish driver's license. You may acquire books regarding Irish driving laws from many post offices and book stores. Newcomers to Ireland should remember that driving is on the left side of the road. Also, driving laws and speed limits are strictly enforced.

- Health insurance — People who are considered to be non-nationals are not covered by the State National Health plan. It is therefore vital that you arrange healthcare coverage while you are in Ireland, until you can obtain coverage in the State Plan. Check with a representative of your current health plan. If he or she can't help you, check with your travel agent. Travel agents can often arrange coverage for you.

- Currency — Ireland's currency is the Punt, which is equal to 100 pence. Punts may be obtained at any bank in Ireland. In the U.S. they may be obtained from the foreign exchange office of most banks. In Ireland, most banks are opened from ten AM to three PM Monday through Friday. Many banks remain open an extra hour on Thursdays. In some very small towns and villages, banking services may be provided only a few days per week. Banks throughout Ireland offer various services and products designed to satisfy virtually all of your banking needs.

- Credit cards — Major credit cards are accepted throughout Ireland, however, VISA and Mastercard are accepted more often than American Express or Diners Club cards.

- Traveler's checks — When traveling, many people prefer to use traveler's checks because of their safety. In Ireland, traveler's checks are readily accepted in cities, however, cash is preferred in rural areas and many towns.

- Post office — Many post offices are open from nine AM to five-thirty PM Monday through Friday, and from nine AM to one PM on Saturdays. Some smaller post offices are closed on Saturdays. The mail in Ireland is efficient, however, it often tends to be slower than the mail service in some other advanced countries.

- Store hours — Most stores are open from nine AM to five-thirty PM Monday through Friday. In large towns and cities, many stores remain open until nine PM on Thursdays and Fridays.

- Night clubs — Many Irish night clubs remain open until two AM. Small bars and pubs often remain open until eleven-thirty PM; Sunday hours are shorter.

- Pets — If you wish to bring a pet (or pets), be aware that all animals coming into Ireland are quarantined for six months.

- Electrical service — Electric service in Ireland is 220 volts. Because plugs are flat with three pins, American appliances need adapters. If you intend to bring any appliances from home, be sure to obtain adapters before attempting to use them.

- Phone service — Phone service in Ireland is quite good, the equal of most advanced nations. For emergency services call 999. For directory assistance call 1190.

- Irish time — Ireland shares Great Britain's time zone, which is five hours ahead of New York, one hour behind Germany and France, and ten hours behind Sydney. Clocks are adjusted one hour ahead in the summer.

- Measurement — Ireland has slowly been changing from the English system of measurement (feet, pounds, miles, etc.) to the Metric system. While many of the new signs for measurement are in Metric units, many of the old ones are still in units of the English system. Food is often measured in either unit, and sometimes both.

- Radio and television networks — Ireland has three national radio stations and many local stations.

There are two national television channels, as well as four British channels, which can be received in much of the country. Cable TV is also available in much of Ireland.

- Newspapers and magazines — You may choose from several national daily and Sunday newspapers in Ireland. Many of these — most notably the *Irish Times* — are considered to practice superior journalism. Both Irish and British tabloids are common in shops. National publications such as *USA Today*, *Time*, and *Newsweek* are available in the major cities, but may be hard to find in some of the smaller towns.

## Recreation and Pleasure

Ireland offers its people countless pastimes and recreations. Newcomers to the country are often surprised at how many exciting activities there are to pursue.

If you like the beach, Ireland has close to 2,000 miles (3,200 km) of coastline, with much of it being clean, sandy beaches. Called *strands* by the residents, many beaches are near bustling resort towns such as Salthill near Galway, Tramore, Bundoran, County Waterford, and County Wexford. Most Irish beaches, however, are kept simple with few amenities — perhaps a pub or small hotel might be nearby. Swimming is popular in July and August, however, beaches are used year-round for walking and jogging.

If you like fine dining, you will not be disappointed in Ireland. Meat, seafood, and dairy products, often with special Irish sauces are important parts of excellent fare. Lamb, pork, lobster, crab, and oysters are also savored Irish dishes. With the coast never more than 90 minutes away, seafood is almost always fresh.

Ireland is known for its pubs. While those who have never visited an Irish pub may mistakenly assume that the place is little more than a bar, Irish pubs are much more. People gather in pubs to share more than liquor — the pub is a gathering place where people talk, laugh, and discuss everything from local gossip to world events. The conversation and relaxation found in pubs can be a most satisfying experience.

For sports enthusiasts, Ireland is a land of plenty. The Irish enjoy a variety of sports, including: bicycling, fishing, golf, hiking, jogging, horse racing, windsurfing, sailing, Gaelic football (similar to rugby), and hurling (similar to lacrosse). Of the many sports, perhaps Ireland's golf courses are best known. Ireland has over 300 golf courses, some of which are world-class in challenge and beauty.

For sightseers, Ireland has enough places to visit to last a lifetime. From marvelous countryside and coasts to Celtic ruins and Norman castles, Ireland is a land of history and tradition. If visiting historical sites, monuments, and museums isn't enough, a number of festivals and special events are held throughout the country in every season. These include horse races, concerts, parades, theater productions, fishing competitions, horse shows, art exhibitions, film festivals, and craft fairs.

Without question, there is plenty to do in Ireland. Newcomers are seldom disappointed.

## Using the Services of Travel Agents

While you can certainly arrange your own travel plans to Ireland, using the services of a reputable travel agent can eliminate or reduce potential problems. Travel agents can arrange for airline flights, hotel bookings, and car rentals, as well as provide helpful information.

When dealing with travel agents, however, be careful that your agent is fully aware of your travel objectives and doesn't influence your plans because he or she has a promotion. If you have a special interest — for instance, if you are traveling to Ireland in hopes of finding a new home — enlist the services of an agent who has expertise and contacts that will aid you in your objective. It will be worth your time to speak with several agents until you find one who will be able to help you.

## The Best Time to Visit Ireland

If you wish to visit Ireland and see the country, be advised that summer is the most popular season for tourists. The weather is the best of the year and the days are long. On the longest days in late June, it doesn't get dark until about ten. Because summer is the height of tourism, prices tend to be high and accommodations, especially at popular places, might be hard to obtain.

Spring and fall — particularly late spring and early fall — are good alternatives. The weather is still very good and the crowds are smaller. Prices, too, are often lower.

If you are considering making Ireland your home, and you plan to make a few trips to the country before resettling, it is wise to travel there in different seasons. This will acquaint you with the overall climate of the country.

# Traveling to Ireland — What to Pack

When considering what type of clothing to pack for Ireland, remember that Ireland is an island and winds from the sea may bring rain at any time. Sometimes, even in summer, the rain can be chilly and soaking. A heavy sweater, raincoat and umbrella are the first items to pack for any season. You should bring heavier clothing for colder seasons. You should also bring at least two pairs of comfortable shoes.

Although the Irish tend to be less formal about attire than many other people, a jacket and tie are required for many bars in the evening, and expensive hotels and restaurants expect their patrons to dress appropriately.

If you must bring medication, either bring enough to last the trip, or be sure to have your doctor write a prescription of the drug in its generic name. The brand names of drugs often vary from country to country. Note: even though you may carry a prescription from your doctor at home, to fill it in Ireland you will need to have an Irish doctor write a new prescription. By having a prescription from your doctor, you will be assured of obtaining the proper medication and dosage. Also, always carry your medications in their original packages or bottles to avoid any confusion with customs agents.

# Getting to Ireland

There are two ways to get to Ireland: by air or sea. If you are traveling to Ireland from Great Britain, either air or sea transportation are practical choices. However, air is the more practical choice for those traveling to Ireland from a distant city or country.

Flights that originate from most major European cities are destined for Dublin Airport, which handles the greatest part of Ireland's air traffic. Flights originating from the U.S. may arrive in Dublin Airport or Shannon Airport, which is near Limerick. Flights from other parts of the world often stop at connecting points such as London and Moscow before flying on to Ireland. Although Dublin Airport and Shannon Airport are the centers for most of the major airlines that fly into Ireland, there are several other airports in the country, but these handle fewer flights. Charter flights often fly into Cork, Kerry Airport, Waterford Airport, and Galway Airport. Ireland is well served by its many airports.

Regular bus service is available from Ireland's major airports, while the smaller airports rely on taxi service. The bus and taxi services are generally efficient and reliable.

For travelers coming to Ireland from Britain or France, a choice of transportation is the ferry. Great Britain has eight ports from which ferries leave for Ireland and France has four. Ireland has six ports which serve ferries. The ferries that travel to Ireland are modern, efficient, and equipped to provide both comfort and security. The ferries feature drive/on drive/ off convenience and offer fine restaurants, lounges, and duty- free shops. (The duty-free shops are available on trips going to Ireland.) Because of their modern design, the ferries are high-speed, making the trip pleasurable and, depending on your point of departure, relatively fast.

All of Ireland's ports offer effective connections for buses and trains, making it easy for travelers to get to nearby cities. From there, it becomes a simple matter to travel to any part of Ireland.

# On the Road in Ireland

If you plan to purchase a home in Ireland, probably the best way to explore the country and visit different towns and counties is by car. Not only will you be able to enjoy Ireland's scenery and historical sites, you will also be able to talk with people around the country. Since it is unlikely that you will have your own car, you will need to rent one. This is of little concern because several international car-rental companies have offices throughout Ireland.      Individuals wishing to rent a car in Ireland must be between the ages of 23 and 70 and must possess a valid driver's license. In some cases, rental companies will make exceptions to the age restrictions.

Because many visitors to Ireland rent cars, it is advisable to arrange a car rental well in advance of your trip. Advance renting can also result in lower rental fees as fees often increase during the summer. You might enlist the aid of a broker company which will obtain for you the best fees for rental cars. Broker companies are known to travel agents and are listed in Irish phone books. Whenever renting a car in Ireland, be sure to check for any hidden costs. Generally, car rental in Ireland includes unlimited mileage, insurance for passengers, theft and fire, but not damage to the car. Before driving a rental car into Northern Ireland, you must inform the company. In many cases additional insurance will be required.

Many of Ireland's roads are low in volume and quiet. Unlike some countries where great highways stretch between cities, Ireland has few major thoroughfares. While driving laws and street signs are similar to those in the U.S. and Great Britain, driving on the left can be somewhat of a challenge for those drivers who have always driven on the right. Caution is essential until the driver becomes familiarized with the new driving perspective. The use of seatbelts is required and children must ride in appropriate safety seats. Roads are posted with speed limits and road signs. Speed limits are shown in miles. Although speed limits vary depending on location, the following examples are rather typical —

- 30 mph (50 kmh) for residential areas.

- 60 mph (95 kmh) rural areas.

- 70 mph (110 kmh) highways.

When first venturing upon Ireland's roads, many visitors are somewhat surprised at their narrowness and winding paths. This is particularly true of Americans, many of whom are used to wide superhighways. While driving on Ireland's roads requires caution for those new to the country, most Irish roads are well paved and safe.

# Ireland — Your New Home

Before buying property and moving to Ireland, you should thoroughly research the country. Visit the places you feel that you might like to live in.

Each of Ireland's cities, towns, villages, and counties has its own charm and character, and you should explore many places to find the one that you will most like. Between Dublin in the east with its Georgian buildings, rich culture, and cosmopolitan airs, Galway City in the west with its port, university, and business, County Donegal in the north with its wild and rugged beauty, and Cork in the south with its bustling business, canals, and bridges lie countless wonderful places to live.

Indeed, Ireland might be one of the world's best places to live. It is a scenic and beautiful country with a strong and growing economy, friendly, English-speaking population, and democratic government. Ireland has tradition and culture, and, perhaps most importantly, a future filled with promise and potential.

# How to Obtain Irish Citizenship

Citizenship comes with rights, privileges, and duties. In some countries the duties far outweigh any rights and privileges citizens enjoy. In others, rights may be well-guarded and institutionalized, but personal freedoms may become hindered and obligations may be onerous. In yet some others, citizenship is hardly worth the bother.

Ireland is a country in which citizenship is valued, and many individuals who were not born in the nation seek to become citizens. Although some people obtain Irish citizenship as a way of honoring their heritage, many others are aware of the benefits that Irish citizenship offers.

An important consideration for many people wishing to obtain Irish citizenship is that citizenship does not come with residency requirements. Moreover, the Irish government does not object to citizens holding dual citizenship, although it is advisable for individuals to thoroughly check their own governments about dual citizenship regulations. The U.S., for example, accepts dual citizenship.

Once Irish citizenship is obtained, an individual enjoys all the rights (and is expected to accept all the duties) of being an Irishman or Irishwoman. He or she enjoys the right to vote in elections, hold an Irish passport, and be entitled to the various benefits provided by the Irish government. Many of these benefits are significant.

While there are requirements that must be satisfied, there are several ways that one may obtain Irish citizenship. The process, though requiring that various criteria be met, is not overly long or frustrating for most people. On the whole, compared to the requirements for obtaining citizenship in many other countries, Irish citizenship is rather easy to secure.

## Why You Should Seek Irish Citizenship

Irish citizenship bestows several important advantages. While many people moving to Ireland seek citizenship because they wish to become a full member of the nation and Irish society, others obtain citizenship for the specific benefits it offers.

Irish citizenship entitles an individual to:

- Travel freely throughout the countries of the EU.

- Live and work in any country of the EU without the need to obtain residence or work permits.

- Buy real estate in any country of the EU.

- Obtain emergency medical care in Ireland at reduced rates.

- Be eligible for a host of additional benefits that fall within the realm of social services. (Note: Some of these benefits are linked to the fact that the individual has paid Irish taxes in the past.)

If you intend to make Ireland your home, even if for only part of the year, obtaining Irish citizenship is advisable.

## Determining Eligibility

The first step to obtaining Irish citizenship is to determine if you are eligible. As provided in the Irish Nationality and Citizenship Act of 1956, there are several routes through which individuals who were born outside of Ireland may gain citizenship, including:

- If either of your parents was born in Ireland, you are considered to be an Irish citizen. To obtain a passport, you need simply to complete and submit a passport application.

- If you have a grandparent who was born in Ireland, or in some cases a great-grandparent who was born in Ireland, you are eligible for Irish citizenship.

- If you are a child of a naturalized Irish citizen (as long as you were born after your parent was naturalized), you are eligible for Irish citizenship.

- If you are a child of an Irish citizen who obtained his or her citizenship through prior registration, you are eligible for Irish citizenship.

- In some cases, if you are the child of a citizen who obtained Irish citizenship through post-nuptial declaration, you may be eligible for Irish citizenship.

# Gathering Documentation

To facilitate the application process for citizenship, you should gather the necessary documents prior to applying. Although the application process is straightforward, lack of documentation will delay the granting of your citizenship and possibly result in denial of your application. Details of requirements are contained in a citizenship application packet, which you can obtain from the Embassy of Ireland located at 2234 Massachusetts Ave., NW, Washington, DC (202-462-3939) or an Irish consulate. While the packet contains specific information, the following guidelines are applicable to most individuals:

- If you are applying for Irish citizenship based on being a grandchild of an Irish-born citizen, you will be required to provide an original and two copies of the following —

    — Birth certificates for your Irish-born grandparent, the parent through whom you are claiming citizenship, and yourself.

    — If they apply, marriage certificates for your grandparent, parent, and yourself.

— Death certificates, if your grandparent or parent is deceased.

- If you are applying for Irish citizenship based on the fact you are a child of a naturalized citizen of Ireland, you will need to provide an original and at least two copies of —

    — The naturalization certificate of the parent on whom you are basing your eligibility for  citizenship.

    — Birth certificates for yourself and your naturalized parent.  It is best to present the the long form of birth certificates. (Generally, baptismal certificates are not accepted in place of birth certificates.)

    — If you or your naturalized parent are married, a marriage certificate for yourself and your  parent.

    — If your naturalized parent is deceased, you   will need to supply the death certificate.

    — A photocopy of your passport.

    — Three additional proofs of identity, including things like a valid driver's license, identification card for employment, or social security card.

— Two identical photos, preferably passport size or larger.

You must be diligent and meticulous in gathering the proper documentation. Many people, for example, don't have birth or marriage certificates of their parents or grandparents. In many cases, particularly if the parents or grandparents are deceased, old, or infirm, they may not know where such documents are and may be of little help in locating them. In these cases it is critical to know where parents or grandparents were born in Ireland. In other cases, it is essential to know where relatives have died. Once you know locations in Ireland, you can contact the record keeper of the area and request what you need. Churches often contain records, too. For most places, when you wish to obtain copies of documents, you will need to make your request in writing. You can obtain the names of agencies that handle vital records by contacting the Irish Embassy. Many counties in Ireland have such agencies. In the U.S. many states maintain vital records agencies or offices that can be of help in tracing parents and grandparents to their original homes.

In cases where an individual doesn't know where his parent or grandparent lived in Ireland, tracking down heritage can be difficult and require great effort and diligence. Persistence is vital.

Obviously, the more information you have, the better your chances for tracing your heritage. Surnames and maiden names are the most practical starting points. Dates and place names are also crucial to an effective search. Often, relatives, friends, and acquaintances can provide helpful information. Former places of work, associations, military service, and immigration records can offer valuable clues.

Because Ireland has more than 70,000 towns and villages, it is most helpful if you can find the one from which your ancestors came. If you can't uncover the town, identifying the county can often be almost as helpful. A variety of genealogical sources are available on-line. Use search terms such as "Ireland, Genealogical Societies." Along with certain groups and organizations, some counties and towns maintain records of family descent.

The Genealogical Project, which is maintained and supported in Ireland by the government, is another potential source. The purpose of the project is to assemble data bases that contain all Irish genealogical sources. Eventually, it is hoped that anyone will be able to search the databases for his or her Irish ancestors, finding out names, where they lived and worked, who they married, and what became of them. Although the project is not complete, you can search an impressive amount of information, focused on specific counties.

A valuable source for Americans is the National Archives in Washington, D.C., from which you can obtain relevant immigration records. The Federal Records Center is yet another potential search site. Catholic churches, particularly those that have been established for a long time, can often provide surprising details about immigrants, including their homes of origins. Even the obituaries of old newspapers can be helpful, because they frequently included the original home of immigrants.

Finally, if you don't have the time or desire to uncover the stones that will lead to your ancestry yourself, you may enlist the services of an individual or company that specializes in genealogical research. For a fee they will attempt to track down your ancestry for you. Before hiring any individual or company to trace your roots, however, you should consult several and compare them for costs as well as the types of searches they conduct. Some of these individuals and companies are more thorough than others. Prices vary, too.

Before embarking upon a search of their ancestry, many people feel that they are at a crossroads. They may continue with their lives as they are, or they may delve into the past and try to uncover the original home of their family. Finding their roots often adds to their understanding of themselves and broadens the way they look at the world.

# Completing the Application for Citizenship

You may apply for citizenship by mail or in person at an Irish Embassy. There is a nominal fee, currently $179 U.S. for adults and $64 for children under 18 years. Note that agencies that supply copies of birth, marriage, and death certificates usually charge fees, too, which will increase your costs somewhat. Nevertheless, the cost of obtaining Irish citizenship is quite a bargain.

When you complete the application for Irish citizenship, be sure to answer all questions and provide all necessary information. Include all necessary documentation as well. Leaving any required information out will result in delays.

For many individuals, the processing of the application takes a few months. If the application is not completed in its entirety, or if documentation is missing, the process can extend to several months. Once citizenship is granted, you can apply for a passport and you will be entitled to all the benefits Irish citizenship offers.

# Dual Citizenship

It is possible to obtain and maintain Irish citizenship, as well as the citizenship of your own country. While some countries do not permit dual citizenship, many others do.

Most countries define citizenship in terms of an individual's descent, birthplace, marriage, and naturalization. This translates to:

- A person is born to parents (one or both of whom) who are citizens of a particular country.

- A person is born on land belonging to or claimed by a particular country.

- A person marries a person who is a citizen of a particular country.

- A person becomes a citizen of a particular country through the process of naturalization.

These are general rules and they vary from country to country. Because an individual may acquire citizenship in different ways, it is possible to obtain citizenship in more than one country. This is called dual (in the case of holding citizenship in two countries), or multiple (when one holds citizenship in several countries).

Countries that frown upon dual citizenship sometimes require that an individual renounce the citizenship he or she holds with another country. Failure to do so can result to thorny legal situations. On the other hand, countries that permit dual citizenship usually don't care that the individual holds citizenship in another country (or countries) as long as he or she lives up to the responsibilities of citizenship. Ireland, for example, doesn't care that an individual holds dual Irish and American citizenship, as long as that individual fulfills his or her obligations to the Irish government. Likewise, the U.S. government isn't concerned if its citizens obtain Irish citizenship, as long as they satisfy their responsibilities to the U.S. government. In such cases, the responsibilities of citizenship generally boil down to payment of proper taxes and the satisfaction of requirements of civic duties. Each country in which citizenship is held generally considers the person a citizen of that country.

Dual citizenship is often an advantage for the individual. Not only can he or she call two countries home, but the person can call on the governments where citizenship is held for protection. For example, a person who holds both U.S. and Irish citizenship has all the rights of Irish citizens in regards to the EU. However, should this individual find himself in trouble in the EU, he may call on the U.S. government for protection. In many cases the U.S. government may exercise greater influence than the Irish government.

For some people, because Ireland maintains double-taxation treaties with many countries throughout the world, obtaining Irish citizenship can reduce their potential tax liability. This, of course, is determined by one's finances and varies from individual to individual.

If you cannot claim Irish citizenship through ancestry or marriage, you may enter the country and apply for permission to stay. You would do this through the local Garda. Permission to stay in Ireland is generally granted with few exceptions. You must be able to support yourself financially, however, and each year you must renew your permit. After five years you can obtain permanent resident status and forego the need to register each year. After seven years you can apply for Irish citizenship, which is usually granted without delay.

For most people who are thinking about moving to Ireland, buying property in the country, or just living in the country part of the year, obtaining Irish citizenship has numerous advantages. Not only do you become entitled to the various benefits available to Irish citizens, you gain easy access to the countries of the EU, and you may qualify for tax advantages.

# Retiring to Ireland

The Republic of Ireland has become one of the world's most desirable retirement destinations in recent years. When you consider the facts, the reasons became clear.

The cost of property in Ireland is extremely reasonable. As noted earlier in this report, from delightful cottages to spacious manors, excellent homes in Ireland are inexpensive when compared to most popular locations around the world. The nation is modern, offering all of the conveniences of any advanced land, yet it possesses marvelous countryside. Its people are warm and friendly, its culture is, without question, unique, its heritage is both profound and mysterious.

Having a population of only 3.6 million makes Ireland a rather empty country. Fewer people results in a slower, more pleasant lifestyle. Ireland is a place where one can truly sit back and enjoy life.

Contrary to what one frequently hears about Northern Ireland — its conflict between Protestants and Catholics —

life in the Republic is tranquil and safe. Indeed, this is one of the principal reasons so many retirees come to Ireland. Safe and clean streets, towns and cities where one is not afraid of his or her neighbors, and an environment that is considered by many to be one of the cleanest — if not the cleanest — in all of Europe are powerful attractions.

No less important for many is Ireland's membership in the EC, which makes it easier for citizens to travel to the member countries. For those individuals who hold travel as a major goal during retirement, Ireland can be the home whose door opens to Europe and beyond.

Finally, the Irish government offers many benefits to its retired citizens. These benefits often extend significantly beyond what are offered in other EC countries. A description of the major benefits follows.

# Free Travel

For individuals living in Ireland who are aged 66 or over, or who are incapacitated, free travel is available. These individuals may use public transportation, as well as designated private bus and ferry services without cost during specific hours. It is noteworthy that there is no limit to the amount of free travel a person may enjoy. A qualifying individual's husband or wife is also entitled to travel without cost when in the company of the qualifying person. Those individuals who qualify for a Companion Free Travel Pass may be accompanied by any person, over 16 years of age, when traveling. This person is entitled to travel free, too.

To be eligible for the free travel benefit, an individual must satisfy the following:

• Be permanently living in Ireland

• Be aged 66 or older

If you are under age 66, you may still qualify. In this case you must:

• Be receiving an Invalidity Pension or Blind Person's Pension from the Department of Social, Community and Family Affairs or satisfy one of the following —

    — Be receiving a social security Invalidity Pension/Benefit or equivalent payment for at least one year from a country included in EC Regulations or a country with which Ireland has signed a bilateral Social Security agreement

— Be receiving workmen's compensation or unemployability supplement with Disablement Pension for at least one year

— Be receiving a Disabled Person's Maintenance Allowance from a Health Board

— Be age 18 or older and registered as a blind person with the National Council/ League of the Blind of Ireland

If you are a widow or widower, age 60 to 65, and your deceased spouse had obtained a Free Travel Pass, and you were residing together before his or her death, you may qualify for a Free Travel Pass of your own. There are some restrictions on this however. To qualify for the pass you must be receiving at least one of the following from the Department of Social, Community and Family Affairs:

• Retirement Pension

• Survivor's Contributory Pension for a Widow or Widower

- Widow's Non-contributory Pension

- Lone Parent's Allowance

- Widow's Pension or Dependent Widower's Pension under the Occupational Injuries Benefits Scheme

Widows and widowers may also be eligible for a Free Travel Pass if they are receiving an equivalent social security pension from a country included in the EC Regulations or from a country with which Ireland has signed a bilateral Social Security agreement.

It is a rather simple procedure to obtain a Free Travel Pass. In some cases, for example, citizens who are receiving a Social Welfare Pension (that makes them eligible) or who are receiving a Disabled Person's Maintenance Allowance from a Health Board are issued a Free Travel Pass automatically. Other people must apply for a pass. Application forms may be obtained from local post offices or social welfare offices.

# Free Electricity Allowance

An allowance is made for free electricity to individuals who are receiving certain social welfare pensions or benefits. The Free Electricity Allowance can result in important yearly savings.

The allowance typically covers 1,500 free units of electricity per year. This amount is broken down into amounts of up to 200 free units of electricity in each two-month billing cycle in the summer and 300 free units in each two-month billing cycle in winter. Up to 600 un-used units may be brought forward to the next billing period.

To be eligible to receive the Free Electricity Allowance, a person must be 66 years old or older and be permanently living at the address to which he or she designates for the allowance. He or she must also be living alone or with family members, an invalid, or a recognized care-giver. (The conditions regarding household members are often relaxed when the homeowner reaches the age of 75.) Furthermore, he or she must be receiving one of the following benefits from the Department of Social, Community and Family Affairs:

- Old Age Pension

- Retirement Pension

- Survivor's Contributory Pension for a Widow or Widower

- Widow's Non-contributory Pension

- Invalidity Pension

- Deserted Wife's Benefit/Allowance

- Prisoner's Wife's Allowance

- Lone Parent's Allowance

- Carer's Allowance

In addition, an individual aged 66 or over may be eligible if he or she is receiving a social security pension from a country included in EC Regulations, or from a country with which Ireland has signed a bilateral Social Security agreement.

*Ireland*

Individuals under the age of 66 may also qualify for this benefit, provided they are receiving one of the following payments:

- A Blind Person's Pension or Invalidity Pension from the Department of Social Welfare.

- Workmen's Compensation or Unemployability Supplement, including Disablement Pension, for at least one year.

- An invalidity pension or benefit for at least one year from a country included in EC Regulations or from a country with which Ireland has signed a bilateral Social Security agreement.

- A Disabled Person's Maintenance Allowance from a Health Board.

Widows and widowers, aged 60 to 65, may also be eligible for a Free Electricity Allowance provided their late husband or wife was receiving the allowance and they were living together. To qualify, widows and widowers must be receiving one of the following payments from the Department of Social, Community and Family Affairs:

- Retirement Pension

- Survivor's Contributory Pension for Widows and Widowers

- Widow's Non-contributory Pension

- Lone Parent's Allowance

- Widow's Pension or Dependent Widower's Pension under Occupational Injuries Benefits Scheme

They may also be eligible if they are receiving a social security pension or benefits from a country included in EC Regulations or from a country with which Ireland has signed a bilateral Social Security agreement.

Applying for a Free Electricity Allowance is a rather straightforward process provided that one of the qualifying requirements is met. Application forms may be obtained at local post offices or social welfare offices.

## Free Natural Gas Allowance

Those people who qualify for the Free Electricity Allowance, but whose homes are connected to a natural gas supply, may be eligible for a Free Natural Gas Allowance instead.  Eligibility requirements are the same as those for the Free Electricity Allowance (see the previous section).  If you satisfy the criteria for free electricity, you will be entitled to the Free Natural Gas Allowance.

The allowance covers up to 2,460 kilowatt hours of natural gas per year.  This total is broken down into amounts of 322 kilowatt hours of natural gas in each two-month billing cycle in the summer and 498 kilowatt hours of natural gas in each two-month billing cycle during the winter.  Up to 967 un-used free kilowatt hours can be brought forward to the next billing period.

Applications for the Free Natural Gas Allowance may be obtained at local post offices or social welfare offices.

# A Host of Additional Benefits

While the Free Travel Pass, Free Electricity Allowance, and Free Natural Gas Allowance are three of the most popular and widely used benefits by retirees, there are many others.  Two of the most important are the National Fuel Scheme and the Living Alone Benefit Allowance.

The National Fuel Scheme is designed to aid households that are unable to pay for their heating needs and are dependent on social welfare or health board payments for a long period.

The Living Alone Benefit Allowance is designed to help those individuals age 66 or over who live alone and who receive payments (in any of several categories) from the Department of Social Welfare.

# Qualifying for a Retirement Pension

Most people who retire to Ireland, and who have recently gained citizenship, or who have not satisfied the country's retirement pension requirements, will not be entitled to a retirement pension. However, there are some noteworthy exceptions that can enable some individuals to qualify for a pro-rated pension that is based on residence and/or social insurance outside of Ireland. Qualification depends on the insurance or pension for which you are eligible in a country included with EC Regulations or a country with which Ireland has signed a bilateral Social Security agreement.

This can be somewhat complicated, obviously, as Ireland, like most countries, is cautious about making exceptions in regards to pension entitlement. However, it is certainly an avenue worth exploring if you feel you may qualify. You may obtain the necessary applications and forms from a local post office or social welfare office.

Without question, Ireland is one of the prime retirement choices for more and more people, not only from Europe and the U.S., but many countries around the world. Few places combine such a green, unpolluted countryside, safe villages, towns, and cities, excellent prices for homes, unparalleled culture and history, warmth and vitality. Ireland is an uncrowded, English-speaking country that is modern, technologically advanced and possesses a growing economy. There is little wonder its attraction for newcomers is so strong.

# At Home in Ireland—Things to Do and Places to Go

For those who call Ireland home, there are countless things to do and places to visit. This chapter details just some places, pleasures, and pastimes that you might enjoy. While many of the places that follow do not have any specific opening times, some do and it is advisable to call ahead before leaving. This will help to reduce the chances that you will arrive at a place when it is closed or times for visiting are restricted.

Whenever visiting just about anywhere in Ireland, it is advisable to dress appropriately and bring along clothing for possible wet weather. May and June tend to be the sunniest and driest months in Ireland, and, throughout the year, rainfall tends to be heavier in the west than in the east. The weather everywhere in the country is generally quite changeable, and it is not uncommon to start a day with bright clear skies only to end with rain, or, conversely, start with a disheartening drizzle to be surprised by sunshine a few hours later.

The Republic of Ireland is divided into four provinces: Connaught, Leinster, Munster, and Ulster. These in turn are divided into 26 counties, numerous villages, towns, and cities. (Nine of the Ulster counties are a part of the United Kingdom.) Each province, and especially the counties, have their own unique characteristics and attractions. Traveling through the country is an enjoyable experience, particularly if one takes time to visit with the locals and explore the area.

Although only about 5% of Irish soil is covered with forests, more than 350 forests are open to the public and provide picnic areas and nature trails. The country, as a whole, because of the wet and mild climate, is covered with a variety of plant life. Ireland is a country where the beauty of nature abounds.

As rich in literature as it is in greenery, Ireland's marvelous literary works can be traced back to the 6th century. Although many of the original works have long been lost, many others have survived, providing a tradition from past to present that rivals the best of virtually any other nation. Much thanks must go to early Christian monks who laboriously copied many of the pre-Christian writings.

One of the earliest writings that has survived is the *Tain Bo Cuailnge*, or *The Cattle Raid of Cooley*, an account of the raid in which Queen Maeve led men of Connaught to capture a prize bull from men of Ulster. From the 12th century comes the *Book of Leinster* which tells of the adventures of Cuchulain and other great heroes of Irish antiquity. *The Annals of the Four Masters*, also written about this time, chronicles much of Irish history to that point.

Many Irish early writings were based wholly or in part on the land's wealth of folklore. Legends, sagas, epics, stories, poems, and sayings are just some of the many types of expression that helped build Irish culture and custom. In the beginning these stories were told by a storyteller, or *seanachie*, who at night would sit beside the fire and repeat stories or valor, wisdom, and tragedy. Such men roamed across Ireland, often telling stories for their supper and a place to sleep. Their ancient stories frequently became the basis of stories, poems, and songs written years later.

Ireland's literary traditions were continued in later centuries by such authors as Jonathan Swift *(Gulliver's Travels)*, George Berkeley (*The Principles of Human Knowledge*), Oliver Goldsmith (*The Vicar of Wakefield*), Oscar Wilde (*The Picture of Dorian Gray*), and George Bernard Shaw (*Pygmalion*). Perhaps Ireland's best known poet is W.B. Yeats, who won the Nobel Prize for Literature in 1923. Another Irish Nobel Prize winner is Samuel Beckett, and although James Joyce never won the prize, his *Ulysses* remains a popular work.

Theater in Ireland is also popular. Several theaters throughout the country host numerous amateur and professional productions, ranging from classic to experimental plays. Along with the traditional theaters, Ireland is filled with repertory groups, outdoor performances, and pub theaters that offer a variety of exhibitions.

Music is yet another popular Irish pastime. Beginning with traditional Irish ballads, reels, and jigs, the spectrum of music includes classical operas, modern jazz, rock, and alternative songs. Music can be heard in just about every part of the country in big halls, small pubs, and on street corners.

For those individuals who find the past interesting, Ireland is rich in history and many ancient monuments and sites are found throughout the country. Archaeological sites are protected by the state and most are open to visitors. Several examples of monuments may be visited, including:

- Dolmens — These tombs are about 4,000 years old. The typical dolmen consists of great stones that support a capstone. An excellent example may be found at Kilternan in County Dublin. Another fine example may be found at Knockeen in County Waterford.

- Passage Graves — These graves usually consist of a central and side chambers with a passage that leads to a mound of earth or stone. Some of these graves date back to about 2,500 B.C. There is evidence that the builders of the graves had an outstanding knowledge of astronomy and geometry, for the graves were apparently designed with knowledge of the winter solstice and are decorated with geometric figures. The Boyne Valley has several good examples of passage graves.

- Round Towers — These towers were likely used as sanctuaries and for refuge. Numerous examples may be found throughout the country.

- Castles — Many castles are found in Ireland. Some date back hundreds of years; many have been restored and are in excellent condition.

- Crosses — Often found at the remains of monasteries, crosses may be large or small and are frequently fashioned from stone. Some are Christian in origin and others date from Celtic times. Many are beautifully detailed with intricate carvings.

Ireland is a country in which a person never runs out of things to visit, explore, or do. Following are some highlights from all parts of the Republic. Since Dublin is the capital city, we'll start there and work our way around the country, region by region.

# Dublin — A City of Bustle, Culture, and Delights

Modern Dublin and its suburbs are home to almost half of Ireland's entire population. The city's residents tend to be young and vibrant, their energy filling the city with an optimistic vitality that many major cities around the world have lost. Dublin has prospered from Ireland's emergence as an economic Celtic tiger, and it is not uncommon for people from the world over to be employees of the many multinational corporations that have opened branches and subsidiaries in the city. Americans, British, Dutch, Germans, French, Asians, and Middle Easterners mix in Dublin's restaurants, shops, and pubs. In some parts of the city, a notable diversified group of people embrace traditional Irish culture.

Always a distinctive feature of Dublin, the city is known for its many pubs. Few remain simple drinking sites anymore, however. Increasingly, pubs are modernizing right along with the city. Modern cafe bars are being opened throughout the city, and new designer pubs stand side by side with the more traditional taverns. For the best in Irish conversation, warmth, and friendliness, a pub is the place to visit.

It is hard to walk down Dublin streets without hearing music. Indeed, music can be found on just about every corner pub, as residents of the city enjoy virtually all kinds of music from traditional Irish ballads and jigs to rock and roll and songs of alternative groups. The recording group U2 is popular throughout the country. Many small pubs and cafes host musical groups for their patrons, however, the Olympia Theater and Temple Bar Music Center are the places to visit if you wish to listen to the performance of major acts, both Irish and international. Along with music performed in pubs and halls, Dublin is also the home of superior classical music and opera. Dance clubs are yet another source of entertainment.

Along with its music, Dublin is known for its literature. Writers of such fame as W.B. Yeats, James Joyce, Sean O'Casey, and Oscar Wilde provide the literary legacy that abounds in Dublin. In bookstores, libraries, and Trinity College, many people spend hours enjoying Dublin's literary flavor. At Trinity College, the *Book of Kells* exhibit is profound.

Fine restaurants and nightclubs are found throughout the city and its suburbs. In the past, most of the cuisine in and around Dublin offered traditional Irish foods, and while traditional restaurants remain, there are many that now serve excellent international fare. Clubs serve food and spirits, and provide dancing well into the late hours.

Some of the most popular sites in Dublin include:

• Trinity College, founded in 1592.

• The National Museum, in which you can examine artifacts from throughout Irish history. Its collections are some of the most impressive in all the world.

• Dublin Writers Museum, considered to be one of Dublin's finest cultural sites. Here you can find some of the original writings, diaries, letters, and other memorabilia from many of Ireland's greatest authors.

• Hugh Lane Municipal Gallery of Modern Art.

• Temple Bar.

- Abbey and Peacock Theatres.

- Olympia Theatre, which is known throughout Europe as one of the best theaters to watch live musical acts.

- Dublin Civic Museum.

- Christ Church Cathedral, founded in 1038. The Normans rebuilt the cathedral in 1169.

- St. Patrick's Cathedral, which was founded in 1190.

- Dublin Castle.

- The National Library.

- The National Gallery, which houses close to 2,000 paintings.

- National Botanic Gardens.

- Phoenix Park, which is the largest park in Europe.

- Sandymount Strand, a marvelous beach.

- Dublin's pubs.

- The Genealogical Office, a must if you intend to conduct research about your Irish ancestors.

- Bewley's Oriental Cafes, of which there are now four sites, specializing in coffee and buns. The original cafe was established in 1842.

- The Wicklow Mountains, just outside of Dublin.

If you prefer sports and outdoor activities to pubs, music, and sightseeing, Dublin has plenty from which you might choose. They range from quiet walks to tough team sports like rugby.

If you prefer the beach, Dublin has three marvelous beaches, called strands: Bull Island, Killiney, and Sandymount Strand. The beach at Killiney is best for swimming, but all three offer breathtaking views and times of solitude for quiet walks.

If you enjoy bicycling, be advised that riding a bike through the city can be dangerous because traffic is often heavy and few streets have bike lanes or shoulders. However, Phoenix Park and several of Dublin's suburbs can be ideal for biking. Not far to the south, the Wicklow Mountains offer rugged countryside that can challenge the most physically fit biker.

Golf is a passion throughout much of Ireland, and it is a popular activity in Dublin. With 30 18-hole courses and several nine-hole courses, a good game of golf is rather easy to arrange.

Tennis is another of Dublin's most popular participant sports. Many parks have fine courts; in addition there are several private tennis clubs.

Horseback riding is yet another favorite pastime of many Dubliners. On the city's outskirts some 20 stables provide mounts and areas for riding. In the city itself, Phoenix Park is a place where one can ride a horse without fear of vehicular traffic. Horseback riding is a popular pursuit throughout much of Ireland, especially in Counties Kildare, Louth, Meath, and Wicklow, which possess fine country for riding.

Akin to horseback riding is horse racing. Truly this is one of the best loved sporting events of the Irish. Dublin and the surrounding area are prime sites for horse racing.

Gaelic games, including Gaelic football and hurling, and rugby and soccer, are featured in sports stadiums in and around Dublin. These games attract large crowds and are popular throughout much of the country.

143

If you would rather shop than participate in sports, Dublin has countless stores, specialty shops, and markets that sell just about any item a shopper might want. The city, in many ways, is a shopper's delight.

Because Dublin is a government, business, and financial center that plays host to global corporations, and because it is a city where past and present come together, it is a unique city. It is a place where just about everyone can find a host of things to do and where one will find it difficult to become bored.

## The Southeast

The counties of Wexford, Carlow, Kilkenny, Tipperary, and Waterford are considered to be a part of Ireland's Southeast. This area of Ireland is unlike the rest of the island. It has the sunniest and mildest climate, and is highlighted by inland meadows and pastures and clean sandy beaches along the coast. Small, idyllic fishing villages dot much of the coastline. Because of its climate and topography, the Southeast is valued as one of Ireland's best vacation spots. Although many visitors come to the area for relaxation, it remains rather undeveloped — an excellent place from which to get away from the rigors of life. Many visitors find the Southeast to be one of Ireland's most pleasant areas.

There is much to do in the Southeast. Popular activities include:

- Hiking. Hiking trails wind through the area, offering scenes of farms, pastures, woods, rivers, and streams. Walking the beaches is a favorite activity for many.

- Horseback riding throughout the countryside or on the beaches. Several stables provide horses for riding at nominal fees.

- Golf at some of Ireland's best courses.

- Greyhound racing. These Irish dogs provide unique excitement when racing; some people feel that Irish greyhounds are world-class in their strength and endurance.

- A variety of spectator sports are held throughout the Southeast, including Gaelic football and hurling.

Some special places to see and visit in the Southeast include:

- Ardmore where you can explore and marvel over early Christian monuments that were built on cliff tops.

- Helvick Head, from which you have a grand view of the sea.

- Youghal Bay, site of sandy beaches.

- Kilkenny City and its restored castle and medieval cathedral.

- The Irish National Heritage Park at Ferrycarrig. This theme park details Irish history through artifacts and replicas.

- Kilmore Quary, site of quaint coastal villages.

- Dunmore Cave, which is a limestone cave containing interesting rock formations. The cave has a long history, having been mentioned in ancient times as the site of heroic struggles.

- The John F. Kennedy Arboretum. In Dunganstown the cottage in which the president's great-grandfather was born still stands.

- The Theatre Royal at Wexford. Also, a major event is the Wexford Opera Festival, held during the last two weeks of October.

- Waterford Castle.

- French Church in Waterford, built in 1240. It is now in ruins, but has an interesting history. Constructed originally for Franciscans, it later provided shelter for Huguenot refugees.

- Waterford Glass, a factory that offers tours demonstrating the various steps of glass production.

- St. Patrick's Well, a site for pilgrims in Tipperary.

- The Rock of Cashel. A popular tourist site, the rock is similar to a great mound that rises about 200 feet from the flat stretch of land that surrounds it. Irish legend claims that the devil is responsible for the rock.

- The countless restaurants and pubs in the region.

# The Southwest

The Southwest, comprising Cork, Killarney, Kerry, and Shannon, is one of the most picturesque regions of all Ireland. Mountains, fertile fields and farms, lakes, rivers, and wonderful coast, all enwrapped within one of Ireland's milder climates, make this region one of Ireland's best.

The region boasts Ireland's second and third largest cities: Cork and Limerick. Although they are rather large by Irish standards, they retain all the amenities that come with an unhurried, uncongested lifestyle. In short, they are cities — offering fine restaurants, numerous pubs, a nightlife, shops, and amusements — yet enjoy a small-town atmosphere.

There is plenty to do throughout this region. Because of the area's excellent farms, restaurants serve meals that rival the best of anywhere in Ireland. Pubs offer not only friendly conversation and fine spirits, they provide a place for bands to entertain their customers. The area is known for its music — everything from traditional Irish folk ballads to modern rock and jazz.

There are many places to see and things to do in the Southwest, including:

- Fishing in the sea or in the region's many lakes and rivers. Salmon and trout fishing are popular. Deep sea fishing, and angling along the coast are likewise enjoyed by many.

- Golf. The Southwest contains some of Ireland's best courses.

- Hiking, in country that many find to have some of the best trails in Ireland. Walking trails make hiking easy, although there are areas of wilderness that will test the stamina of the most avid hikers.

- Bicycling in an area known for its hills.

Some special places to visit in the Southwest include:

- Killarney's many lakes.

- Bunratty Castle.

- St. John's Cathedral in Limerick. The cathedral has the highest spire in Ireland.

- Limerick Museum, which contains historical items and informative materials about Limerick's past.

- Cush, where you can study ancient burial mounds.

- Lough Gur, site of various prehistoric monuments including cairns, dolmens, stone forts, and pillar stones.

- Ballycasey Crafts Centre, where you can find various craft products for sale.

- Hunt Museum, which houses Celtic artifacts.

- Kinsale, a port town with a fort dating from the 17th century.

- Blarney Castle and the famous Blarney Stone. Kiss the stone and legend says that you will acquire the Irish "gift of gab."

- Fota Wildlife Park, which is home to a variety of animals including giraffes, cheetahs, kangaroos, monkeys, emus, and flamingos.

- The Ring of Kerry, offering incredible coastline and mountains.

- The Beara Peninsula.

- The Dingle Peninsula.

- Innisfallen Island.

- St. Mary's Cathedral, the oldest cathedral in Limerick. It is noteworthy that Limerick is mostly a Catholic city and St. Mary's is a Protestant religious site.

- The many restaurants, pubs, and halls that are found throughout the Southwest.

# Western Ireland

Much of Western Ireland remains the center of old Irish traditions and values. Throughout much of the island's history, while other areas of Ireland were assaulted by Vikings, Normans, and British, much of the west remained free from domination. Even today, more people in the West speak Gaelic than in any other region of Ireland. Small towns and farms highlight land that is both rugged and beautiful. Perhaps more than any other part of Ireland, the West might be described as undeveloped, a land that remains much as it was years ago.

This is not to say that the counties and towns of Western Ireland have little to offer. Galway, the major town of the region, is considered to be the center of Ireland's traditional music. Indeed, this region has much to share, including:

- Fishing in some of the finest rivers and lakes in all of Europe. Deep-sea fishing is also enjoyed from coastal towns.

- Sailing, especially on Galway Bay during the summer months.

- Hiking in a country that is both challenging and inspiring. Large areas of low population make this region one of Ireland's best for hiking and exploring.

- Horseracing. A variety of races are held throughout the year in the region.

- Golf on many excellent courses.

Following are special places to visit in Western Ireland:

- Connemara National Park.

- The Aran Islands. Most of the population here speaks Gaelic and has not changed their way of life much in generations.

- Dromoland Castle, which can trace its ownership back to the descendants of Brian Boru, the famous king of Ireland.

- Ballinalacken Castle.

- The Matchmaking Festival at Lisdoonvarna during late September. Traditionally, the purpose of the festival was to help farmer bachelors find wives.

- Coole Park, the site of the home of W.B. Yeats's patron, the Lady Augusta Gregory.

- Thoor Ballylee, a 14th century Norman tower once owned by Yeats. It is near Coole Park.

- Dunguaire Castle, which is said to be on the site of a 7th century castle, built by the King of Connaught.

- University College Galway. The library contains impressive materials on the Celtic language and and history.

- The Galway Arts Festival, held during the last two weeks in July, is a celebration that includes a parade, music, drama, and films.

- The Druid Theater Company inGalway, known for its quality productions.

153

- Ballybrit Racecourse, which holds various races, perhaps the most famous of which is the Galway Race Week which is a major social event of the area.

- The various pubs, restaurants, and shops that give this region its own particular flair and flavor.

# Ireland's Northwest

With rugged coastlines, long stretches of pristine beaches, and mountains dissected by valleys, ridges, and cliffs, the northwestern region of Ireland is one of the country's most wild and beautiful. Sligo and Donegal dominate this region, which offers jagged coast and peninsulas to farms tucked beneath the mountains. The towering beauty of the land is a strong draw for vacationers, whose numbers, during the months of July and August, detract somewhat from the finest places this region has to offer. However, there are still plenty of places to go and things to do in the Northwest.

On your trip to this region, you may indulge yourself in any of the following:

- Fishing, particularly deep-sea angling. The Northwest is prized for its fishing festivals.

- Surfing. Along the Sligo and South Donegal coasts the Atlantic waves make for delightful and challenging surfing.

- Golf. Like just about everywhere else in Ireland, you are never far from quality courses.

- Hiking. The Northwest offers many trails for hiking, including some rather demanding ones through the mountains.

In addition, there are several places to visit and sites to see in the Northwest, including:

- Sligo Town.

- Donegal Town.

- Donegal Castle, the ruins of which date from the 15th century.

- Crownarad Mountain, offering spectacular views.

- Killybegs, a delightful and postcard-like fishing port.

- Creevykeel, which is a burial site over 5,000 years old.

- Ards Forest Park, where you can visit sites dating to prehistory.

- Glebe House and Gallery, in which you can see works by Picasso and Jack Yeats, as well local artists.

- Yeats Gallery Library Building, in which you will find a significant collection of works by Jack B. Yeats.

- Markree Castle, which dates from 1640.

- Hawk's Well Theater in Sligo, which is well known for providing a stage for both amateur and professional companies.

- Carrowmore Megaliths, site of more than 60 tombs dating to the Bronze Age.

- Ballyshannon Dram Festival, held in early June.

- Ballyshannon Music Festival. A folk-music event held during the beginning of August.

- Donegal Craft Village.

- Donegal Castle, which dates from the late 15th century.

- Horn Head, one of the most stunning of the headlands of County Donegal.

- Glenveagh National Park, which includes some of the wildest land in Donegal, including mountains, forests, and lakes.

- Inishowen Peninsula. This is the northernmost peninsula of Ireland, with coastal lands rising up to interior mountains.

- Malin Point. The northernmost point of Ireland, quite impressive as it juts out into the sea.

## Ireland's Midlands

The counties, towns, and villages that comprise Ireland's Midlands make up the center of the country in more than mere geography. It is places including these — Offaly, Roscommon, Longford, Cavan, Monaghan, Westmeath, Kildare, Kilkenny, Thurles, and Carlow — that possess much of what is considered to be quintessential Irish. Broad rivers, including the famed Shannon, wide lakes, and myriad ponds highlight the plains that provide a picture of green hills and meadows filled with wildflowers. The Midlands are a place of quiet towns and farms where neighbors know each other and some families go back generations.

Despite their bucolic setting, the Midlands offer a variety of activities and pastimes, including:

- Hiking and walking along delightful country roads, among virgin land around lakes and ponds, and through the trails of forest parks.

- Dining in small restaurants and eateries throughout the area. While you won't find fancy, expensive restaurants in the Midlands, you will find plenty of good food including beef and fish.

- Bicycling along the many country roads.

- Fishing in the many rivers, lakes, and ponds. A variety of fish may be caught in the waters of the Midlands, and fishermen from all over Ireland come here to try to their luck. The area hosts various fishing festivals and tournaments, which can become events in themselves.

- Boating on the many waterways. Several companies rent craft for fishing, cruising through the Midlands, and simply sailing.

- Golfing. Like just about everywhere else, golf courses are found at several locations in the Midlands.

Some special places to see in the Midlands:

- Clonmacnoise, one of Ireland's most famous monastic settlements, originally founded between 543 and 549.

- Lough Key Forest Park, which includes a bog garden, cypress grove, and interesting ruins.

- Cavan, which is famous for its crystal.

- Headford/Deerpark, which offers walking trails through woodlands.

- Kilkenny Castle, originally built in the 12th century.

- Kilkenny Design Workshops, offering displaysof glassware, woven products, and jewelry.

- Emo Court and Gardens, a large country home that is open to the public.

- Killykeen Forest Park, which offers nature trails, beautiful country, horseback riding, bicycling, and boating.

- Silvermine Mountains, where you will find excellent areas to hike and climb.

- The various restaurants, historical sites, and waterways of the region.

Without question, there is much for you to do in Ireland. The country is one of the truly fine places to live. Unspoiled land, clean waters, and a friendly people make Ireland an ideal home. For those individuals who relocate to Ireland, the country promises to be a journey of discovery and enjoyment.

# About the Author

Over the past 25 years, Adam Starchild has been the author of over two dozen books, and hundreds of magazine articles, primarily on business and finance. His articles have appeared in a wide range of publications around the world -- including Business Credit, Euromoney, Finance, The Financial Planner, International Living, Offshore Financial Review, Reason, Tax Planning International, The Bull & Bear, Trust & Estates, and many more.

Now semi-retired, he was the president of an international consulting group specializing in banking, finance and the development of new businesses, including tourist enterprises. He has owned and operated travel agencies, travel wholesalers, and tour operators.

Although this formidable testimony to expertise in his field, plus his current preoccupation with other books-in-progress, would not seem to leave time for a well-rounded existence, Starchild has won two Presidential Sports Awards and written several cookbooks, and is currently involved in a number of personal charitable projects.

His personal website is at http://www.adamstarchild.com/

www.ingramcontent.com/pod-product-compliance
Lightning Source LLC
Chambersburg PA
CBHW031810190326
41518CB00006B/278